Robert Beauchamp

Elaine de Kooning

Willem de Kooning

Robert Goodnough

Grace Hartigan

Lester Johnson

Alex Katz

George McNeil

Jan Müller

Jackson Pollock

Fairfield Porter

Larry Rivers

Bob Thompson

This exhibition and catalog are dedicated to the memory of

Thomas B. Hess

John Bernard Myers

Frank O'Hara

Organized by

Paul Schimmel

Chief Curator

Newport Harbor Art Museum

and

Judith E. Stein

Associate Curator

Pennsylvania Academy of the Fine Arts

Essayists

Klaus Kertess

Carter Ratcliff

Paul Schimmel

Judith E. Stein

the
FIGURATIVE *FIFTIES*

I new york
figurative
expressionism

Newport Harbor Art Museum · Newport Beach, California

Rizzoli · New York

This book is published in conjunction with the exhibition *The Figurative Fifties: New York Figurative Expressionism*, organized by the Newport Harbor Art Museum, Newport Beach, California with the assistance and cooperation of the Pennsylvania Academy of the Fine Arts, Philadelphia, Pennsylvania.

First published in the United States of America in 1988 by the Newport Harbor Art Museum, 850 San Clemente Drive, Newport Beach, California 92660, and Rizzoli International Publications, Inc., 597 Fifth Avenue, New York, New York 10017.

Exhibition Tour:

Newport Harbor Art Museum
Newport Beach, California
July 19-September 18, 1988

The exhibition in Newport Beach has been made possible by a generous gift from The Irvine Company, Newport Beach, California. Additional funding was provided by the National Endowment for the Arts, a federal agency.

Pennsylvania Academy of the Fine Arts
Philadelphia, Pennsylvania
October 12-December 31, 1988

The exhibition in Philadelphia has been made possible by a generous gift from CIGNA Foundation and The Pew Charitable Trusts.

McNay Art Museum
San Antonio, Texas
February 15-April 30, 1989

The exhibition in San Antonio has been made possible by a generous gift from anonymous donors.

The exhibition has been made possible by a generous gift from The Irvine Company, Newport Beach, California. Additional funding was provided by the National Endowment for the Arts, a federal agency.

Editor: Sue Henger
Design: Lilli Cristin
Printed and bound in Japan.

Library of Congress Cataloging-in-Publication Data

The Figurative Fifties
Bibliography: p.
1. Figurative expressionism—New York (N.Y.)—Exhibitions. 2. Painting, American—New York (N.Y.)—Exhibitions. 3. Painting, Modern—20th century—New York (N.Y.)—Exhibitions. 4. New York school of art—Exhibitions. I. Schimmel, Paul, 1954- II. Stein, Judith E. III. Newport Harbor Art Museum.
ND235.N45F54 1988   759.147'074019496   87-73222
ISBN 0-8478-0942-0 (Rizzoli)
ISBN 0-917439-12-5 (pbk. : NHAM)

Contents

The Irvine Company entered into a ten-year commitment to underwrite Newport Harbor Art Museum exhibitions in 1984, when it sponsored *Action/Presicion: The New Direction in New York, 1955-60*. The Museum's ability to contribute to art historical scholarship by reexamining the formative years of the New York School was underscored in the 1986 exhibition *The Interpretive Link: Abstract Surrealism into Abstract Expressionism, Works on Paper 1938-48*.

With *The Figurative Fifties: New York Figurative Expressionism*, The Irvine Company is pleased to complete its support of an important trilogy of exhibitions that will be remembered for their fresh interpretations of a dynamic period in modern art.

We look forward to equally challenging and thoughtful presentations over the remaining five years of our exhibition sponsorship commitment and to sharing the Museum's cultural contributions with audiences throughout the country.

Donald L. Bren
Chairman

 THE IRVINE COMPANY

Foreword

The organization and production of *Action/Precision: The New Direction in New York, 1955-60* by the Newport Harbor Art Museum in 1984 began our exploration into American art of the 1950s. That detailed review of six second-generation abstract expressionist artists of the New York School led to an additional study into the traditions and history of contemporary art in our 1986 exhibition *The Interpretive Link: Abstract Surrealism into Abstract Expressionism, Works on Paper, 1938-1948.*

This exhibition, *The Figurative Fifties: New York Figurative Expressionism,* explores the other side of the expressionist tradition. While abstract expressionism had its proponents in the 1950s, so did figurative expressionism. In this exhibition both are brought together. It is gratifying to see the scholarship demonstrated in this exhibition and publication, augmenting that of *Action Precision* and *The Interpretive Link*, and to see the culmination of over five years of focused, concentrated work by our staff.

Paul Schimmel, Chief Curator at the Newport Habor Art Museum, has been the driving force behind all three exhibitions. With *The Figurative Fifties* the Newport Harbor Art Museum has had the superlative assistance of Judith Stein, Associate Curator at the Pennsylvania Academy of the Fine Arts, in organizing and producing the show. Both have contributed their knowledge and expertise to this catalog. Without them this exhibition would not have achieved its present scope and quality.

My thanks go to Linda Bantel, Director of the Pennsylvania Academy, for her assistance and cooperation not only in supporting the conception and formation of the exhibition, but for placing *The Figurative Fifties* at the Academy. We are also grateful to John Palmer Leeper, Director of the McNay Art Museum, San Antonio, Texas for participating in the circulation of this exhibition.

Exhibitions of this nature are always costly, particularly in light of the spiraling value of American art of this period. I am grateful to the National Endowment for the Arts, a federal agency, for their support. Without question, Donald L. Bren, Chariman of The Irvine Company, Newport Beach, and the board, officers and employees of the company have as enthusiastically supported this third in the series of exhibitions exploring the New York School as they have the previous two. My deepest words of appreciation go to The Irvine Company; without their contributions our examination of American art of the 1950s would have remained a dream.

Finally, I am grateful to our Board of Trustees and staff, who in addition to sharing the dream, committed their energy to making *The Figurative Fifties* a reality, and to the President and Board of Trustees of the Pennsylvania Academy of the Fine Arts, who supported the project conceptually and strategically from its inception. ■

Kevin E. Consey
Director

9

Lenders to the Exhibition

Private Collections

Robert Beauchamp, New York
Arthur M. Bullowa, New York
Elaine de Kooning, New York
Dr. and Mrs. Martin L. Gecht, Chicago
Barbara K. Goldman, Birmingham, Michigan
Richard and Mary L. Gray, Chicago
Lester Johnson, Greenwich, Connecticut
Judith and Mitchell Kramer, Jenkintown, Pennsylvania

Luke Luyckx, New York
George McNeil, Brooklyn, New York
James and Mari Michener
Mr. and Mrs. John T. Ordeman, St. Petersburg, Florida
Sondra and Alfred Ordover, New York
Katherine Porter, Atlanta, Georgia
Eve Propp, New York
Larry Rivers, New York

Mr. and Mrs. John Martin Shea, California
Ashby McCulloch Sutherland, San Antonio, Texas
Lyda A. Quinn Thomas, Galveston, Texas
Howard and Barbara Wise, New York
Virginia and Bagley Wright, Seattle, Washington

Institutions

Albright-Knox Art Gallery, Buffalo, New York
Archer M. Huntington Art Gallery, The University of Texas at Austin
Art Gallery of Ontario, Toronto
The Brooklyn Museum, Brooklyn, New York
The Chrysler Museum, Norfolk, Virginia
The Corcoran Gallery of Art, Washington, D.C.
Solomon R. Guggenheim Museum, New York
Hirshhorn Museum and Sculpture Garden, Smithsonian Institution, Washington, D.C.

Lannan Foundation, Los Angeles
The Metropolitan Museum of Art, New York
The Minneapolis Institute of Arts, Minneapolis
Modern Art Museum of Fort Worth, Texas
The Museum of Modern Art, New York
National Museum of American Art, Smithsonian Institutition, Washington, D.C.
Nebraska Art Association, Lincoln
The Nelson-Atkins Museum of Art, Kansas City, Missouri
Oklahoma Art Center, Oklahoma City, Oklahoma
The Parrish Art Museum, Southampton, New York

Seattle Art Museum, Seattle, Washington
Sheldon Memorial Art Gallery, University of Nebraska at Lincoln
The Toledo Museum of Art, Toledo, Ohio
Vassar College Art Gallery, Poughkeepsie, New York
Wadsworth Atheneum, Hartford, Connecticut
Walker Art Center, Minneapolis
Weatherspoon Art Gallery, The University of North Carolina at Greensboro
Whitney Museum of American Art, New York

Galleries

Vivian Horan Fine Art, New York
Hirschl & Adler Modern, New York
Robert Miller Gallery, New York
Allan Stone Gallery, New York

Acknowledgments

The Figurative Fifties: New York Figurative Expressionism would never have been possible without the generous cooperation, enthusiasm and dedication of many collectors, dealers, museum professionals, art historians and, most importantly, the artists. It is the artists themselves who must be acknowledged first for having created the magnificent legacy of figurative painting during the 1950s and early 1960s. At a time when abstraction was the prevailing movement, these artists continued along their own paths of discovery, creating a figurative alternative that ranged from near abstraction to representation.

Robert Beauchamp, Elaine de Kooning, Willem de Kooning, Robert Goodnough, Grace Hartigan, Lester Johnson, Alex Katz, George McNeil, and Larry Rivers cooperated in all aspects of organizing this exhibition. The curators benefited from their direct involvement, their suggestions of works, and their willingness to be interviewed. The families of Jan Müller, Fairfield Porter and Bob Thompson willingly provided information about the artists' working methods and concerns. We gratefully acknowledge Dody Müller for information about her husband, Jan Müller; Anne and Elizabeth Porter for information on Fairfield Porter; and Carol Thompson for information on her husband, Bob Thompson. We also thank Leslie De Troy, assistant to Lester Johnson, Diana Molinari, assistant to Larry Rivers, and Edvard Lieber, assistant to the de Koonings.

To the numerous lenders to the exhibition, our heartfelt thanks for agreeing to participate. Without their generosity, this endeavor could never have been realized. The increasing importance, fragile nature and large scale of many of the works in this exhibition have made the contributions of the collectors, museums, galleries and artists all the more significant. The museums and foundations that have been generous in lending many works to the exhibition include Albright-Knox Art Gallery, Douglas G. Schultz, Director, Micheal G. Auping, Chief Curator, and Alba Priore, Registrar for Outgoing Loans; Art Gallery of Ontario, Roald Nasgaard, Chief Curator, and Catherine Spence, Registrar; Archer M. Huntington Art Gallery, Eric S. McCready, Director, Patricia Hendricks, Associate Curator and Loan Officer, and Sue Ellen Jeffers, Registrar; The Brooklyn Museum, Robert T. Buck, Director, Charlotta Kotik, Curator of Contemporary Art, and Barbara LaSalle, Registrar; The Chrysler Museum, David W. Steadman, Director, and Katherine Jordan, Registrar; The Corcoran Gallery of Art, Jane Livingston, Associate Director, William B. Bodine, Jr., Assistant Director for Curatorial Affairs, and Cindy Rom, Registrar; Solomon R. Guggenheim Museum, Thomas M. Messer, Director, Diane Waldman, Deputy Director, and Jane Rubin, Registrar; Hirshhorn Museum and Sculpture Garden, James T. Demetrion, Director, Ned Rifkin, Curator of Exhibitions, Phyllis Rosenzweig, Associate Curator, and Peggy Dong, Registrar; the Lannan Foundation, Bonnie Clearwater, Director, Art Programs, and Cynthia Nalevanko, Registrar; The Metropolitan Museum of Art, William S. Lieberman, Chairman, 20th Century Art, Lowery Sims, Associate Curator, and Ida Balboul, 20th Century Research; The Minneapolis Institute of Arts, Michael Conforti, Chief Curator and Bell Memorial Curator of Decorative Art and Sculpture, and Karen Duncan, Associate Registrar; Modern Art Museum of Fort Worth, E.A. Carmean, Director, and Rachel Blackburn-Wright, Registrar; The Museum of Modern Art, New York, Richard E. Oldenburg, Director, Linda Shearer, Curator, and Elouise Ricciardelli, Registrar; the National Museum of American Art, Charles C. Eldredge, Director, Harry Rand, Curator, Painting and Sculpture, and Melissa Kroning, Assistant Registrar; The Nelson-Atkins Museum of Art, Marc F. Wilson, Director, and Anne Erbacher, Registrar; Oklahoma Art Center, Mary Delle Stelzer, Director, and Sue Scott, Director, Eduction Programs and marketing; The Parrish Art Museum, Trudy C. Kramer, Director, and Alicia Longwell, Registrar; Seattle Art Museum, Arnold Jolles, Director, Patterson Sims, Associate Director, Collections and Exhibitions, and Paula Wolf, Assistant Registrar; Sheldon Memorial Art Gallery, George W. Neubert, Director, and Ruth York, Registrar; The Toledo Museum of Art, Roger Mandle, Director, Robert F. Phillips, Curator of Contemporary Art, and Pat Whitesides, Registrar; Vassar College Art Gallery, Joan Mickelson Lukach, Director, and Dennis Anderson, Registrar; Wadsworth Atheneum, Andrea Miller-Keller, Curator of Contemporary Art and Acting Chief Curator, and David Parrish, Registrar; Walker Art Center, Martin Friedman, Director, and Carrie de Cato, Registrar; Weatherspoon Art Gallery, James E. Tucker, Curator, and Eric Lawling, Registrar; Whitney Museum of American Art, Thomas N. Armstrong III, Director, and Roberta LeMay, Acting Assistant Registrar, Permanent Collection.

Galleries have been an important resource both in the research and for loans to this exhibition. The galleries that assisted with loans include Allan Stone Gallery, Allan Stone and Joan Wolff; Hirschl & Adler Modern, Donald McKinney, Director; Robert Miller Gallery, John Cheim, Director, and Nathan Kernan; Vivian Horan Fine Art, Vivian Horan, Director, and Diane Reed.

We are especially grateful to the private collectors and the participating artists themselves for allowing works from their ersonal collections to be exhibited in public. These lenders include Robert Beauchamp, Arthur M. Bullowa, Elaine de Kooning, Dr. and Mrs. Martin L. Gecht, Barbara K. Goldman, Richard and Mary L. Gray, Lester Johnson, Mitchell and Judith Kramer, Luke Luyckx, George McNeil, Mr. and Mrs. John T. Ordeman, Mr. and Mrs. Alfred Ordover, Katherine Porter, Eve Propp, Larry Rivers, Mr. and Mrs. John Martin Shea, Ashby McCulloch Sutherland, Lyda A. Quinn Thomas, Marcia Weisman, Howard and Barbara Wise, Virginia and Bagley Wright, and others who prefer to remain anonymous.

The curators wish to express their appreciation to the many individuals who have helped enrich their knowledge of figurative expressionism in the 1950s. Norman Bluhm, Alfred Leslie, Jay Milder and Robert de Niro gave generously of their time and information, as did Yvonne Andersen and Val Falcone, Lawrence Campbell, Katherine Kuh, Martica Sawin, and Prescott Schutz. We are particularly indebted to collectors Frances Pernas and Horace Richter, who shared our belief in the need for *The Figurative Fifties* exhibition, and to artist Wolf Kahn, who was instrumental in introducing us to each other. We are grateful to Julian Weissman of M. Knoedler & Co., Suzanne Vanderwoude, of Vanderwoude Tananbaum Gallery, Susanne Hilberry of Hilberry Gallery, Howard Scott of M-13 Gallery, Patricia Shippee of Shippee Gallery, Gary Lejeski of Tower Gallery, Putter Pence of Pence Gallery, Jill Weinberg of Xavier Fourcade, Inc., Dody Müller of David Anderson Gallery, and David Moos, Director, Walter Moos Gallery. Richard Bellamy of Oil and Steel Gallery, Martha Henry, formerly of Richard Green Gallery, and John Lee of Tibor de Nagy Gallery also gave freely of their time.

We also gained valuable insights from conversations with Dore Ashton, Martha Baer, Janet Fish, Audrey Flack, Marc Freidus, Allan Frumkin, Harry Gaugh, Sandy Gilbert, Red Grooms, Bruce Guenther, Bud Holland, Sam Hunter, and the late John Bernard Myers.

This catalog represents the contributions of many, including the critical essayists, the entry essayists and researchers, and of course the artists themselves. We are especially grateful to those art historians who contributed to the catalog. Klaus Kertess and Carter Ratcliff joined the curators in contributing major essays. Specific texts on each of the artists were contributed by B.H. Friedman, Helen A. Harrison, Judith Higgins, Jeffrey Hoffeld, April Kingsley, Elizabeth Langhorne, Robert Mattison, Kenworth Moffett, Brian O'Doherty, Irving Sandler, and Judith Wilson. To all of these writers, we express our appreciation for their insightful commentaries.

The catalog has been compiled and edited by Sue Henger, Museum Editor, and her assistant, Peter Kosenko. Ursula R. Cyga merits thanks for assistance with proofreading. Lilli Cristin is recognized for her sensitive, sophisticated design for this catalog and the earlier catalogs in this series. To William Dworkin, Lauren Shakley and Solveig Williams of Rizzoli International we express our deep appreciation for their early enthusiasm and commitment to copublish this exhibition catalog.

The curators wish to acknowledge the sustained commitment and integral role of the Pennsylvania Academy of the Fine Arts in the developmental phase of this exhibition. To Linda Bantel, Director, and Frank Goodyear, President, we owe particular appreciation. We also wish to thank Ann Classen, Curatorial Assistant, Marietta Bushnell, Librarian, Regina Neu, former Curator of Education, Elaine Breslow, Director of Development, Lainie Lomenzo, Director of Marketing, and Lucinda Costin, Public Relations Officer for their work on *The Figurative Fifties*.

We are grateful also to the McNay Art Museum for having agreed early on to particiapte in this exhibition.

The curators are especially grateful to Kevin E. Consey, Director of the Newport Harbor Art Museum. His support over the past six years for this exhibition and its predecessors *Action/Precision* and *The Interpretive Link* has provided an opportunity to investigate fully the New York School movement.

We are grateful to the Newport Harbor Art Museum's interns Ned Elliott and Katherine Hovde for providing research, coordination and compilation of material for this exhibition; Betsy Severance, Registrar, for registration and the complex logistics involved in crating, shipping and insuring the works of art; Lorraine Dukes, Assistant to the Chief Curator, for handling much of the communication with the museum lenders, artists and participating venues; Richard Tellinghuisen, Director of Operations and Brian Gray, Exhibition Designer, for designing and installing the exhibition at the Newport Harbor Art Museum; Ellen Breitman, Curator of Education, and Karin Schnell, Education Assistant, for their diligent efforts to provide educational programs of lectures, docent tours and supplementary educational events. Thanks are also due to Jane Piasecki, Associate Director; and Margie Shackelford, Director of Development, Kathleen Costello, Associate Director of Development, and Kathy Bryant, Public Relations Officer, for their contributions in the areas of funding and public relations. ∎

Paul Schimmel
Judith Stein

Introduction

The 1950s was an explosive period in American art, a time when New York became the preeminent center of the world's avant-garde. *The Figurative Fifties: New York figurative Expressionism* presents eighty-one figurative paintings and drawings by thirteen diverse New York artists who countered the prevailing abstract mode to work with the figure.

This exhibition begins in 1949 with Willem de Kooning's first experiments in the "Woman" series and extends into the early sixties to track the mature manifestations of figuration in the work of Lester Johnson, Alex Katz, George McNeil, Robert Goodnough, Robert Beauchamp and Bob Thompson.

The artists who comprise *The Figurative Fifties* fall into several subcategories: de Kooning and Pollock, first-generation abstract expressionist masters, worked in an abstract figurative mode that used the figure as an armature or framework on which to build their gesturally expressionistic canvases. Another tactic was followed by Larry Rivers and Grace Hartigan, who relied initially on the influences of Old Master and history painting in the early fifties. Elaine de Kooning also worked within the figurative mode in the first half of the fifties. Both she and Fairfield Porter shared an interest in representational portraiture. Jan Müller, a critical force in this exhibition, invented an allegorical, mythical painting that brought stylistic elements of the German expressionists to the heroic scale of the abstract expressionists. In the wake of Müller's breakthrough, Robert Beauchamp and Bob Thompson worked with subjects drawn from religious, mythic and allegorical sources.

By the end of the fifties, another generation of artists moved into a figurative mode. They include Alex Katz, Lester Johnson, George McNeil and Robert Goodnough. Katz's accurate representation of family members and friends aligns him with Porter and Elaine de Kooning. Johnson, McNeil and Goodnough, who came from an abstract background, increasingly included figurative elements in their work at this time.

As curators, we have sought to rectify the lingering impression that New York avant-garde painters eschewed the figure in the fifties and to refute the implication that artists who used the body as form and subject produced work that was the less for doing so. We have interpreted figuration as signifying human form and have selected artists whose work reflects the style and methods of abstract expressionism.

In concentrating on artists who turned to the figure in the 1950s, we have had to exclude more those painters who had already associated themselves within the figurative mode and who remained relatively unaffected by the abstract expressionists; thus Alice Neel, the Soyer Brothers, Earl Kirkham, Morris Kantor and Leonard Baskin are not part of this exhibition. Similarly, we have not included such well-known fifties painters as Wolf Kahn, Nell Blaine, Jane Freilicher and Jane Wilson, who, although influenced by abstract expressionsim, made their major contribution in the area of landscape, nor painters such as Felix Pasilis, who focused on still lifes. Neither have we included such artists as Robert Motherwell, Franz Kline, Philip Guston, Lee Krasner, or Alfred Leslie, who were associated with the abstract expressionists and who hinted at the figure but for whom have also not been included in this exhibition since the figure played a relatively minor role in their work in the 1950s.

This exhibition will also help to rectify a misconception that figuration flourished only in the hinterlands of Chicago, San Francisco, and in Europe. The fact that 1950s Bay Area figurative artists Richard Diebenkorn, Elmer Bischoff, David Park, Nathan Oliviera are more widely known than many of the New York figurative painters is due primarily to the overwhelming critical hold of abstract expressionism on the East Coast.

Unlike the second-generation abstract expressionists, who were a coherent group of artists of the same generation whose work was stylistically similar, the artists in *The Figurative Fifties* worked in a far broader range of styles. Nonetheless they acknowledged and, in some cases, took a leadership role in the abstract expressionist movement. The artists in this exhibition were not working in a cultural vacuum. As friends they were part of the extended family of the abstract expressionists and readily recognized the importance of their achievements.

The Figurative Fifties is the collaborative project of two curators. Paul Schimmel came to work on this aspect of the fifties following his earlier investigations in the exhibitions *Action/Precision* and *The Interpretive Link*, organized by the Newport Harbor Art Museum. Judith Stein was drawn to this material by way of searching out the sources of Red Groom's early figurative style for *Red Grooms: A Retrospective, 1956-1984*, an exhibition generated by the Pennsylvania Academy of the Fine Arts. Both curators shared a sense of the importance of isolating the accomplishments of the New York School figurative expressionists as a group distinct from the Bay Area painters, who have long been recognized as a significant presence in the history of American art. The painters who comprise *The Figurative Fifties* have never been the sole focus of a museum exhibition as such.

In the late fifties and early sixties, museums in New York and elsewhere mounted a range of exhibitions documenting fifties expressionist figuration.[1] In the intervening decades, abstract expressionism has so colored the definition of the fifties that the contributions of the figurative expressionists have been obscured. The evolution of taste and the reemergence of an expressionist esthetic in the early eighties have surely influenced the timing of the present exhibition. Twenty years ago artist and critic Gabriel Laderman, in a review of the 1967 Schoelkopf Gallery exhibition *Figurative Painting of the Fifties*, expressed his wish for a larger show on the subject with several major paintings from each artist, "the kind of show only a museum could successfully mount."[2] With *The Figurative Fifties*, the public now has the opportunity to assess the achievements of these thirteen New York School painters who worked with the figure, not to contradict abstraction but to extend it.

The figure in the twentieth century is an enduring legacy. The works in this exhibition take their rightful place between the German and French figurative expressionists of the twenties and thirties and the pop painters of the sixties. The Figurative Fifties provides an historical context for neo-expressionists of the early eighties. ∎

Paul Schimmel
Judith Stein

Notes

1. See Judith Stein's essay "Figuring Out the Fifties," in this catalog, for a description of these exhibitions.

2. Gabriel Laderman, "Figurative Painting of the Fifties," *Artforum* (January 1968), p. 57.

The Other Tradition

Klaus Kertess

Betrayal. Betrayal was what many of Willem de Kooning's fellow abstract expressionists felt upon viewing his 1953 Janis Gallery exhibition entitled "Paintings on the Theme of Woman." The viscous stops, starts and erasures of the five "Woman" paintings (begun in 1950) brought a turbulent new body to de Kooning's painting — a more urgent physicality than was present in the overall pulsation of the intertwining layers of organic slabs that populated the black and white abstractions in de Kooning's much-acclaimed first exhibition in 1948. For many the ferociously vacillating figures were a retrograde intrusion upon, rather than an embodiment of, the epic struggle with the acts of making that de Kooning's marks sought to render visible. It was assumed that he, like his peers Pollock, Newman, Rothko and Still, would have completely and willingly surrendered the figure to the inexorable flow of the new American abstraction. Indeed, despite the extremely different solutions of its various practitioners, so monolithic had abstract expressionism's recently achieved hegemony become that the doors of history seemed tightly shut behind it. Influences critical to the development of these radical new abstractionists had been so completely internalized as to be erased by the all-encompassing existential present. De Kooning, probably the least programmatic of his generation, was virtually alone in his visible continuation of a dialogue with the past — from Titian to Rubens, Rembrandt, Van Gogh and the cubists' grid. For him abstraction and figuration were not mutually exclusive, just as easel scale and mural scale were not.

One of the primary achievements of the abstract expressionist painters was their radical reinvention of the radiant, purely optical physicality and the procedural clarity so prevalent in works of late nineteenth-century painters like Van Gogh and Monet. With the advent of cubism, this opticality more or less lapsed from mainstream modernism: cubism, constructivism, purism, and surrealism all depended on a linear/planar or illusionistically rendered tactility (Kandinsky's early abstractions are obviously the major exceptions). Ironically, the figure that became such anathema had often been the primary guardian and carrier of the painterliness that returned to the forefront in the fifties. But the role such figurative artists as Nolde, Soutine and Dubuffet may have had in the formation of this new painting was soon suppressed by the cult of heroic originality that quickly surrounded abstract expressionism.

While deflating its mythic heroics, succeeding generations of painters continued to press abstract expressionism's implacable, frontal overallness forward to create a more totally self-reflexive neutrality. They had neither need nor desire to rescue the figure from its exile. Pop art served only further to alienate the figure from painting by mechanically reproducing its media images.

Revolutions have never been distinguished by their fairness. The monumental purge and reconstitution of painting's means and ends that took place in New York in the late forties and early fifties may well have required the banishment of the figure in order to consolidate its painterly power. It must be remembered that although John Marin was considered America's greatest painter in the forties, since the twenties America had only grudgingly begun accepting modernism. The figure in its role as harbinger of conservatism became an obvious target for abstractionist defensiveness — a defensiveness prone to blur the vast distinctions between figurative painters and to exaggerate the differences between the figurative and the nonfigurative. It was not until the late sixties and early seventies that the figure was permitted to return from exile and even to make claims to centrality. Now, abstraction itself took part in the rehabilitation. The prince of self-reflexiveness, Frank Stella, began to investigate the compositional complexities of premodernist figure painting; and younger artists like Stephen Mueller and Bill Jensen rejected minimalism and field painting in favor of an openly and richly referential abstract figuration. In 1968 the riotous, comic grotesques that began to emerge out of the gummy viscosity of Philip Guston's once abstract strokes led a new parade of figurative painterliness and expressiveness that was joined by younger artists such as Joe Zucker and Neil Jenney and the born-again expressionist Malcolm Morley. Soon a new generation of German expressionists made their mark, and the kaleidoscope of history could be turned to refocus on the figure's past in the twentieth century and before. It is this refocusing that this essay wishes briefly to sketch, in order to build some context for reconsidering the New York painterly figurative work included in this exhibition. This is a story of revision, not of discovery.

The transition from the nineteenth to the twentieth century, in art, is perhaps most clearly marked by the Salon d'Automne exhibition of 1905 in Paris, where the newly formed group

Henri Mattise
Pianist and Checker Players, 1924
oil on canvas
29 x 36⅜ inches
National Gallery of Art, Washington;
Collection of Mr. and Mrs. Paul Mellon

Pierre Bonnard
The Breakfast Room, c. 1930-31
oil on canvas
62⅞ x 44⅞ inches
Collection The Museum of Modern Art,
New York, given anonymously

dubbed the Fauves was given center stage. Led by Matisse, Vlaminck and Derain, they extended the lessons of Cézanne, Van Gogh, and Seurat into a brash polyphony that liberated color of all its remaining descriptive chores. By 1909, in such paintings as *La Danse*, Matisse had turned Cézanne's monumental, shifting, planar architecture into a flatter, open flow of color/light that achieves a nearly abstract, lyric euphoria. These works, together with the more starkly reductive succeeding paintings (e.g., *View of Notre Dame*, 1914) are among the masterpieces of early modernism and were crucial in influencing the broad fields of color created by Newman and Rothko in the late forties and early fifties. Modernism was less comfortable with the seemingly more representational interiors, odalisques and still lifes Matisse painted between 1916 and 1930. Here Matisse extended seventeenth-century genre painting into the twentieth; but he brought to it an astounding abstract compositional complexity and a mediterranean light and hedonism that rivaled the more Nordic restraint of Vermeer. Matisse's many representations of the female in these paintings at once celebrate and sublimate sensuality into pure icons of light. While never totally ignored, these paintings have only recently been accorded their rightful prominence in Matisse's and the twentieth century's achievement. Their smooth spread of color and their elaboration of a compositional structure that embraces the figure so figuratively and abstractly provided valuable lessons, in the late 1940s and early 1950s, to a young group of painters, namely, Alex Katz, Jane Freilicher, and Larry Rivers, seeking a new formal validity for the figure.

These three painters, as well as their older colleague Fairfield Porter, also found much to admire in the late works of Bonnard and Vuillard. In 1889, together with Maurice Denis, Bonnard and Vuillard had helped found the Nabis. Influenced by Gauguin and by the decorative flatness and radical cropping of Japanese woodblock prints, these artists fueled painting's push towards abstraction. After 1905, however, both Bonnard and Vuillard turned to a more resolutely representational mode of painting that earned them Maurice Denis's disdain and the dreaded label of conservatism. Like Matisse between 1916 and 1930, they celebrated the theater of the everyday with interiors and still lifes, but their paintings have both a more insistent surface and a greater fidelity to appearance. Vuillard's subdued color, blurred profiles, discreet but forthright physicality and low-key compositional finesse were particularly important to

Emil Nolde
Christ Among the Children, 1910
oil on canvas
34⅛ x 41⅞ inches
Collection The Museum of Modern Art,
New York, Gift of Dr. W.R. Valentiner

Pablo Picasso
First Steps, 1943
oil on canvas
51¼ x 38¼ inches
Collection Yale University Art Gallery, Gift
of Stephen C. Clark, B.A. 1903

the early development of Freilicher and Porter. After 1925 Bonnard devoted himself primarily to the nude. More openly sensuous than Matisse's nudes and bathed in a dense fluttering of acid color and diffused light, these paintings have a blazing depth far less conventional than many an orthodox modernist work.

If the Fauves' chromatic pyrotechnics and distorted simplifiction of form seemed to further the subjugation of the subject to abstract, formal concerns, the German artists who were simultaneously forming Die Bruecke in 1905 subjugated formal concerns to the subject. Led by Ernst Ludwig Kirchner, including Otto Mueller, Erich Heckel, Max Pechstein and Karl Schmidt-Rottluff, and joined for a year and a half in 1906 by Emil Nolde, the artists of Die Bruecke were more influenced by Van Gogh's urgency and Gauguin's linear flatness than by Cézanne. German medieval art, African sculpture and Edvard Munch's traumatized psychosexuality helped compound their emotive intensity. Their subjects ranged from the plight of urban living to primitive arcadia, the battle of the sexes and deep Christian religiosity. The intuitive fervor of their paint often paralleled the fervor of their subjects—most notably in the flaming, exotic lushness of Nolde's frontally packed and frenzied compositions devoted to the life of Christ. Most recently revived by such German artists as Georg Baselitz and Rainer Fetting, this group provided models for the more gestural side of painterly expressionism (both abstract and figurative) and left open the possibility of incorporating a wide variety of narrative subject matter, despite the rising tide of abstraction.

The African art that influenced Kirchner's angular distortions and that would continue to be a psychological and formal model for much twentieth-century primitivism was even more crucial to the beginnings of Picasso's more analytical disjunctions, leading him into cubism and the full liberation of form from appearance that largely made abstraction possible. In Picasso's seminal *Demoiselles d'Avignon* (1907), the two central figures still retain a relative wholeness that recalls the long tradition of placid European odalisques from Titian to late Renoir. But the flanking figures, especially the two on the right, begin to surrender their bodies to overlapping, planar breaks and slides. Their African-masked faces give them a confrontational power that shifts from the purely formal to the ferocious; these are the earth goddesses and whores who would increasingly replace the

Max Beckmann
Blindman's Buff, 1945
oil on canvas
left panel: 73 ½ x 40 inches
center panel: 81¼ x 91¼ inches
right panel: 73⅞ x 41¾ inches
Collection The Minneapolis Institute of Arts,
Gift of Mr. and Mrs. Donald Winston

Georges Rouault
The Old King, 1916-36
oil on canvas
30¼ x 21¼ inches
Collection The Carnegie Museum of Art,
Patrons Art Fund, 40.1

more bucolic nudes of the past and ultimately lead to de Kooning's "Woman" paintings. In the thirties, Picasso would himself turn the cool calculation of his earlier cubism to more expressive ends with his endlessly varied paintings of women—sleeping, weeping, sensual or lugubrious. These paintings, as well as *Guernica* (1937) and his many paintings of mythological subjects, were seminal to Pollock's development, as well as to de Kooning's and so many other artists'.

Cubism's dematerialization of form lent itself as readily to spiritual and expressive ends as to more formal analytical ones. Franz Marc and August Macke, who, among others, joined Kandinsky in the founding of the Blaue Reiter group in 1911, merged the lessons of fauvism with cubism and Delaunay to form crystalline hymns of Nordic spiritualism similar to, if not as masterful or encyclopedic as, those of their Blaue Reiter compatriot Paul Klee.

Cubism had a more peripheral effect on Max Beckmann; together with the shattering effects of World War I, it helped free him from his early romantically representational mode. Beckmann's claustrophobically compressed and disjointed space became the stage for enigmatic allegories of human violence; bars and/or radically tilted space often repel the viewer from tableaux incorporating bound women, torturers, blindfolded actors, clowns, and assorted grotesques. His great triptychs of the thirties combine a translucent clarity of color, a masterly physicality of paint and line, and a compelling compositional structure to bestow a powerful monumentality to his depictions of the culture self-destructing around him. His figures are less radically distorted than Picasso's figures in *Guernica*, but his color is more complex, his paint richer, and his fractured compositions at least as strong. The breadth, depth, and ambition of Beckmann's figurative expressionism remains all but unparalleled in twentieth-century painting. Although his direct influence is hard to track (Alice Neel was clearly influenced by Beckmann), he was widely admired and exhibited in the United States, where he spent the last three years of his life (1947-1950).

Like his peer Beckmann, the Austrian Oskar Kokoschka pursued an independent development, but one that totally abjured cubism in favor of a more turbulent baroque painterliness.

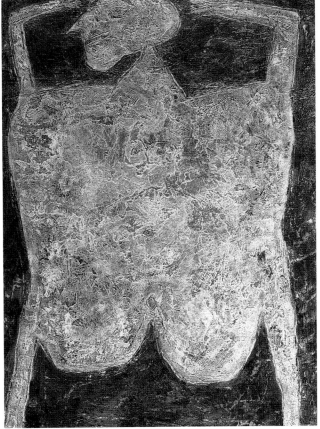

Moving in 1910-20 from the hothouse nervousness of Klimt to a more robust restlessness, Kokoschka often painted figures stigmatized by their sexuality. While remaining relatively true to appearances, Kokoschka nevertheless succeeded in raising yet another hand in favor of a nonmodernist opticality.

Painterly expressiveness was not the exclusive domain of Germanic artists. In Paris, Georges Rouault and Chaim Soutine added to the figurative ferment. Rouault was the favorite pupil of his own and Matisse's teacher, Gustave Moreau, and he exhibited with the Fauves in 1905. However, while, like the Fauves, he revered Cézanne, his pathos-packed works of whores, clowns, and the Passion of Christ grew out of his deep Catholic conviction. His paintings in oil, especially after 1918, were created with a summary directness and volatility of surface and color that matches the intensity of Nolde. The rich impasto, the light-giving brilliance of Rouault's carmines and blues, and the hieratic, thickly outlined contours look back both to Rembrandt and to medieval stained glass (Rouault served an apprenticeship in a stained glass workshop as a young student).

Soutine had no interest in Rouault's sociopolitical and religious subject matter, but he shared in his love of Rembrandt (especially the *Slaughtered Ox*, which Soutine could see in the Louvre after his arrival in Paris from Russia in 1912). Starting with a group of landscapes painted in southern France between 1919 and 1923, Soutine unfurled an astounding fury of paint. The single figures that populate many of his paintings are enveloped, ravaged and ravished by eruptions of viscous liquidity. This agitated physicality stands, temporally and stylistically, midway between Van Gogh and de Kooning, who was one of Soutine's strong admirers in the thirties.

Unlike Rouault and Soutine, the younger Jean Dubuffet sought to turn his back completely on the tradition of Western painting. Like the future abstract expressionists, he placed a strong emphasis on the materiality of his medium (often thickened and coarsened with sand) and on intuitively direct means that would totally short-circuit cultivated Western notions of drawing and painting. After several fitful starts and stops, he developed an art in the forties that reflected his interest in the art of the untrained (mostly of the clinically insane). His exuberant colony of infantilely linear, leering, cartoon-like figures that

were often incised into the monochrome impasto of his surface, may well have influenced Pollock's similarly painted sgraffito paintings of the mid-forties. Certainly they had an impact on George McNeil's later, more colorful carnival of figures of paint.

Mention must be made parenthetically here of Alberto Giacometti's extraordinary figurative sculpture of the forties. Eaten away by space, his eviscerated spectres partake of the "formlessness" so crucial to the developing abstract expressionists; but they are also consummate expressions of the existential dilemma of the figure—in art and in life—in the mid-twentieth century.

If no attention has been paid thus far to the figure in American painting, it is largely because the American figure remained more bound to a nineteenth-century realist tradition, updated more by subject matter than by expressive means of painting. From the time of Robert Henri's and John Sloan's founding of The Eight (in 1908) to the regionalists and social realists of the thirties and Edward Hopper and the Soyers in the forties, the figure remained attached to relatively conventionally depicted space and place, although Reginald Marsh's raunchy scruffiness is not so far removed from Larry Rivers's painting from the early fifties onward. With the exception of Maurice Prendergast, most of the American painters who entered into a dialogue with Parisian modernism from the early twentieth century on (John Marin, Georgia O'Keeffe, Marsden Hartley, Max Weber, the Synchronists, et al.) were more committed to landscape and/or abstraction. The highly visible presence of the Mexicans Diego Rivera and Jose Clemente Orozco in the thirties held out new hope for figurative growth. Although Rivera's mural projects became the model for the WPA murals, and although he had a strong influence on Thomas Hart Benton and many other regionalists and realists, his Italian fresco-inspired scale proved to be most fertile for the development of abstract expressionism (just as the radical experimentation with industrial materials and techniques Orozco encouraged in his New York workshop held out its primary promise to the young Pollock).

Ironically, in the late thirties and forties, on the eve of the new abstraction's purge of figuration and its rise to all-encompassing prominence, the figure began to acquire a new and forceful

Milton Avery
Two Figures at Desk, 1944
oil on canvas
48 x 32 inches
Collection Neuberger Museum, State
University of New York at Purchase, gift
of Roy R. Neuberger

vigor. Max Weber, who had earlier been the most militant of America's first modernists, blossomed into a figurative expressionist, creating thinly but actively painted compositions indebted to Picasso's Ingresque drawings of the twenties, and primarily devoted to Jewish themes. Like Weber, one of the first to convert Cézanne and cubism to his own ends in the teens, Marsden Hartley now added the figure to the brooding Ryderesque landscapes that had dominated his work since the early thirties. The stark dignity and directness of Hartley's folk-art-inspired figures have an intensity that matches their often Christian subject matter. Their power must be seen in the context of the best of Hartley's European and American peers.

The myth and spirituality so important to many figurative and abstract painters in the forties played no role in the lyric restraint of Milton Avery's landscapes and figure paintings. His flattened compositions pare down and mute Matisse's hedonism. After 1940 Avery's suppression of light and dark contrasts and his increasingly saturated and nonassociative color influenced the development of the abstraction of his two friends Mark Rothko and Adolph Gottlieb, as well as that of Barnett Newman. The breadth of Avery's openness and reductiveness was also important to Alex Katz as he began to approach a more monumental scale, and his expressive color is singular in the development of American painting.

Edwin Dickinson
Evangeline, 1942
oil on canvas
20 x 23 inches
Courtesy Hirschl and Adler Modern,
New York

The visible clarity and directness of procedures of making so important to American painting since the late forties got off to an early start in Edwin Dickinson's small seascape and portrait paintings of the mid-thirties on. Their blurred, luminous liquidity gives a mercurial materiality to the paint and the painted alike. Dickinson's energized, whited-out light made a strong impression on Willem de Kooning; and his evanescence is reflected in Elaine de Kooning's portraits. These Whistler-inspired intimate and spontaneous paintings, together with Dickinson's more metaphysically plotted and entranced lunar tableaux form a body of work that has yet to receive its proper due. Dickinson, too, gives ample evidence that the dialogue between expressive paint and the figure could more than survive the increasing pressures of abstraction and could even teach it a thing or two.

If, as this writer and others believe, the abstraction invented in

New York in the late forties was and remains American painting's strongest achievement, there is, nonetheless, scant reason for the eclipse that many of the artists' achievements so cursorily charted above has endured. None of these artists was totally forgotten, certainly not Picasso and Matisse, but many were prematurely stuffed into history's file for the obsolete. All were known to the artists who reached their maturity in the late forties and early fifties. The German expressionists, who in Germany were punished with censorship and ultimately with the prohibition and destruction (in 1937) of their work, were promoted by Alfred Barr at New York's newly created Museum of Modern Art—starting with the 1931 exhibition "German Painting and Sculpture." Barr was particularly supportive of Beckmann, whose stay in the States was preceded by a number of solo exhibitions at New York's Buchholz Gallery. The Modern also hosted Kokoschka's traveling retrospective in 1948; and Rouault was the subject of two exhibitions, one in 1945 and one in 1953. In 1950 Soutine was given a posthumous retrospective. Dubuffet had his first American solo exhibition at the Pierre Matisse Gallery in 1947; Giacometti followed there in 1948 and had a retrospective at the Guggenheim Museum in 1955. Rivera, whose muralizing in Mexico and the United States was attended with acclaim and notoriety, was the subject of the Museum of Modern Art's second retrospective, in 1932 (Matisse was the subject of the first).

Recent exhibitions of late Bonnard, Beckmann, Rivera, Avery, and Hartley have revived and reactivated the lapsed viability of their paintings and helped to catalyze a continuing dialogue with younger artists. Nolde, Rouault, and Soutine are over-ripe for review as the figure continues its search for an identity in paint. ■

Selfhood Paints a Self-Portrait

Fifties Figuration in New
York and Elsewhere

Carter Ratcliff

Favorite Painting in the Metropolitan

"these are the stairs
from *Funny Face*"

but I would like to see
the three Zenobius bits
before I die of the heat
or you die of the denim
or we fight it out without
lances in the obscure public

"I don't think Houdon
does the trick"

and I could walk through exchanging with you through the
exchanging universe tears
of regretless interest tears of
fun and everything being temporary
right where it seems so permanent

"when I saw you coming
I forgot all about Breughel"

no we love us still hanging
around the paintings Richard Burton
waves through de Kooning the
Wild West rides up out of the Pollock
and a Fragonard smiles no pinker
than your left ear, no bigger either

"let's go by my place
before the movies"

I don't really care
if I have a standard or not
or a backless coat of mail
since I never intend to back
up or out of this
whether not is something

"but I think there's
a lot of sin going on"

a long wait in the lists
and the full Courbets like
snow falling over piles of shit
such sadness, you love all
the Annunciations you are feeling
very Sunday take axe to palm

"they weren't just Madonnas,
they were skies!"

so if we take it all down
and put it all up again differently
it will be the same elsewhere
changed as, if we changed we would
hate each other so we don't change
each other or others would love us

"oh shit! a run"

I see the Bellini mirror and this
time you follow me seeing me in it
first, the perfect image of my
existence with the sky above
me which has never frowned on me
in any dream of your knowledge

Frank O'Hara*

In Frank O'Hara's habitat, meaning was conveyed by gestures—verbal, painterly, flamboyant even when oblique. A heated, sometimes frantic place, this sector of the Manhattan art world was central in the 1950s. It steadily became more marginal as coolness swept through the sixties in a triple wave. First came the deadpan of pop art, then minimalism's industrial sheen, and next the color-field painters' devotion to theory. By the time of his death in 1966, O'Hara's stylishness was out of style. Two decades later, his jittery refinement seems almost as unrecoverable as the melancholy of T.S. Eliot's "Wasteland." Yet the effort to evoke O'Hara's sensibility will help us understand the figures that appeared in New York painting in the 1950s—among them, Elaine de Kooning's athletes; Robert Goodnough's saurian creatures, which evolved into many things, from cowboys to Laocoön; and Grace Hartigan's nudes and carnival celebrants.

These artists nominated themselves the preservers and elaborators of action painting, as Harold Rosenberg called it. Arguing in support of Jackson Pollock, Willem de Kooning, Franz Kline and a few others, Rosenberg concluded that the vicissitudes of the avant-garde alienated the serious artist from all but an audience of peers. Preserving their integrity by signaling their estrangement, ambitious painters confronted "in daily practice the problematic nature of modern individuality." It had become "appropriate to speak of the canvas as an arena" where the artist sought a confirmation of selfhood in acts of painterly desperation.

Rosenberg envisioned action painting as a lonely struggle, pitting the isolated individual against the void of an empty canvas. Never proscribing figurative images, he nonetheless assumed that "the demolition of existing values" would mitigate

25

against them.[1] In art-world usage, the phrase "action painting" was roughly synonymous with "abstract expressionism." Yet second-generation action painters like Elaine de Kooning and Robert Goodnough chafed at this synonymy and the assumptions behind it. For them, action in the Rosenbergian "arena" was too stark, too lonely, too neatly symmetrical a face-off between artist and medium. Disinclined to treat the figure as an impediment on its way to obsolescence, they turned painting into a three-way struggle between the painter, painting as painterly gesture, and painting as a picture of identifiable things. Their figures gave a social flavor to a crisis that Rosenberg had defined in part as painting's failure to engage society.

Recognizably human images did not win a large, reliable audience for the work of the second-generation action painters. They were almost as isolated from the larger culture as their predecessors had been. Moreover, they came under attack from some artists and critics who argued that painting betrayed its own nature by trying to recover what its alienation had inspired it to jettison.[2] Figurative action painters put the opposing argument, though not without doubts. Their figures often had to fight for visibility amid waves and tangles of choking, smothering pigment. By 1958 painting-as-gesture and painting-as-picturing were so intimately entwined and so notoriously at odds that, with the briefest of hints, the poet James Schuyler could invoke these two notions of the medium as scaffolding for an *Art News* review. On the one hand, Schuyler saw the legible images in Lester Johnson's new canvases as sign of "forethought"; on the other, he noted a surface "alive" with a painterly spontaneity that "forethought" supposedly precludes. Johnson, said Schuyler, had loosed a "rare bird, Action Painting with nameable subject matter."[3] This mixture of the painterly and the recognizable overflowed New York galleries in the 1950s, as the present exhibition demonstrates. Yet Schuyler greeted its appearance in Johnson's art as something precious and rarely glimpsed. Even as it proliferated, the painterly figure looked like an endangered species.

Frank O'Hara's faith in the quick glance and the improvised gesture required throwaway poems like "Favorite Painting in the Metropolitan," which is more a record of art-talk than an exercise in the high poetics of his most ambitious works. Insofar as "Favorite Painting" is verse, it is a love poem. He addresses it

not only to the unnamed person who dashes with him up the grand staircase of The Metropolitan Museum in New York ("'these are the stairs from *Funny Face*'"), but to the paintings they see in the galleries (canvases by Gustave Courbet, Jean Fragonard, Willem de Kooning). Iconography enchants him ("the three Zenobius bits," "the Annunciations"), at least when he sees it at high speed. Either the poem's narrator or his companion is bored by the marble-white propriety of 18th-century neoclassicism ("'I don't think Houdon does the trick'"), though a pun about standards (at once esthetic and heraldic) enlivens the dullness of chain mail and armor. Pieter Breughel is worth a mention, but only as the exemplar of a stolid greatness forgotten when one of the poem's two characters catches the day's first, exciting glimpse of the other.

Willem de Kooning has said, "Content is a glimpse of something, an encounter like a flash."[4] His feel for the speed of such encounters led the artist to talk of a "slipping glimpse"[5] that induces ambiguity in what is seen, mixing figure and ground, people and their surroundings. In 1953, with *Woman I* recently completed and *Woman as Landscape* two years in the future, de Kooning said, "The landscape is in the Woman . . . and there is Woman in the landscapes."[6] One moment, O'Hara's "Favorite Painting" makes an equation between an artwork and a body part ("A Fragonard…no pinker/ than your left ear, no bigger either"); a moment later, it finds memories of a movie in another object of art ("Richard Burton/ waves through de Kooning"). New York poet and painter alike assemble images from slipping glimpses of the kind that, early in the century, produced the cubists' ellipses, shuffled planes, and visual puns.

Guided by Cézanne's example, cubism made painting into a negotiation with the visible world. The upshot of the process is an image that stamps what is seen with marks of the artist's idiosyncratic seeing. This is different from a Romantic's attempt to impose a transcendent vision on familiar appearances, for that is a spirtual, even quasi-religious effort to persuade mundane phenomena to reveal numinous underpinnings. One thinks of William Blake and the later work of J.M.W. Turner. By contrast, the early, topographically accurate Turner defined mimesis — the imitation of nature — in a spirit of modern empiricism. Positing art as an objectively accurate investigation of facts led to realism, then naturalism, and such counter-developments as cubism, which refuses to exclude the seer from the seen. The cubists and their heirs among New York School painters are secular artists who accept the very texture of the ordinary, yet hold out for the right to inflect that texture with memories of their medium's past and the urgent pressures of immediate experience.[7] Such inflections can overwhelm the recognizable, producing the implicitly figurative abstractions one sees in Willem de Kooning's fragmented forms of the late 1940s.

In 1950 he cut lipsticked smiles from full-color ads and pasted them to the canvas. Around these readymade images the ragged but enveloping unities of the Woman paintings coalesced. Collage is an extreme instance of a familiar device: the inter-pretable image, suddenly intruded, that tips a painting's balance away from abstraction. This intrusive image need not be made of pasted paper, and in the New York fifties usually wasn't. During mid-decade, Grace Hartigan's "slipping glimpse" brought recognizable bits of the world into paintings that look, at first glance, abstract. As her action painting loosened its grip on the identifiable, James Schuyler described a batch of new paintings as if they were still figurative. The "color acidities" of *Dublin* (1958-59), he wrote, are "urban colors, like weathered and brutal hoardings, more kinds of brick than there are roses, cheap ready-to-wear drying and fading on clotheslines." The blue of the equally abstract *Bray* (1959?) "flows all through it, unwatery but changeable and bold as a deep clear sky reflected in a harbor surface shattered by traffic and a light wind."[8]

Two seasons before, Schuyler charted Elaine de Kooning's swerve toward abstraction in terms that writers of an earlier or a later decade would have reserved for realism: "in their rawness her pictures always have a strong tone of psychological insight and honesty, of knowledge of action: not of how things seem to happen, but actually happen, the discipline of fascinated observation."[9] Reviewing the undeniably abstract works the artist exhibited at the start of the 1960s, Lawrence Campbell wrote that her colors

> do not have "shapes." They are large movements, rushing, gliding, scattering, pouring, a glissade, an excitement of oranges, and a blue which, in such surroundings, takes on a shrill, loud quality, a kind of high-pitched thud, also yellows, alizarins, purples, chartreuse greens and black.[10]

It's not that Campbell sees figures where there are none. Rather, he describes Elaine de Kooning's imagery as if figuration and abstraction were interchangeable options. For this painter, they were. Each had the power to compromise the other, and the resulting impurities could, if encouraged, render critical description ambiguous. Campbell deliberately lets it seem as if his topic has shifted from painting to an explosion of cacophonous sound.

Abstraction carried figurative baggage; figurative images had the volatility of abstraction. In 1959 Frank O'Hara asked Larry Rivers, "Have you ever *invented* a shape in your paintings?"

> *Rivers*: As far as I'm concerned *nothing* makes an invented shape more moving or interesting than a recognizable one. I can't put down on canvas what I can't see. I think of a picture as a smorgasbord of the recognizable. *Interviewer* [O'Hara]: Could you illustrate what you mean? *Rivers*: I may see something—a ribbon, say, and I'll use it to enliven a three-inch area of the canvas. Eventually it may turn into a milk container, a snake or a rectangle.

Rivers's way of talking about his art implies that the ribbon turns into a milk container of its own accord. A playful implica-tion, it is nonetheless strong enough to warrant the conclusion that he invites the world to shape the look of his art even as his art shapes the world's look.

At Hans Hofmann's school, Rivers learned a version of late cubism. Asked by O'Hara if he had ever had a "'de Kooning' period," Rivers said, "Yes, but don't tell anyone."[12] Resisting Picasso and Willem de Kooning with the help of Pierre Bonnard and Henri Matisse, Rivers only occasionally qualified as a figurative action painter. Nor does the label always fit Fairfield Porter, whose elegantly blotted manner pays homage to Edouard Vuillard rather than Bonnard. Yet the brash Rivers and the restrained Porter share with de Kooning and the younger action painters the slipping glimpse that questions the differences between abstract and figurative images and blurs the lines of command linking artist and motif. Sometimes it looks as if Porter or Rivers has left it up to the viewer to decide whether a bit of brushwork has the weight of the recognizable or the floating versatility of sheer paint. The painter cedes to each member of the audience the final say about meaning, or so it seems, though this abdication may be only the subtlest of the illusions generated by pictorial slippage. One can't be sure who is in charge. Roles shift, as in O'Hara's "Favorite Painting," where jump starts and quick stops make it impossible to know who says what or which remark is backed by what portion of which elusive figure's personal authority. Up for grabs, the self may be an inward core of being, a reflection of contemporary urban style, a refraction of high-art traditions, or all these and more.

In 1954 Larry Rivers painted Frank O'Hara frontally nude, combat boots on his feet, and his hands, with fingers laced, resting upon his head. Here Rivers makes a grandiose gesture of sacrificing himself to the alien muses of pornography and Théodore Géricault, the Romantic painter who supplied this figure with its pose and the image with its darkly melodramatic palette. Three years earlier, Rivers had redone Gustave Courbet's *Burial at Ornans* (1850) à la Chaim Soutine. He returned to Courbet in 1956, this time to reinvent *The Painter in His Studio* (1855). Like its source, Rivers's *The Studio* (cat. 72) arranges figures in a wide tableau. His cast of characters is more domestic than Courbet's and his manner far less ponderous. In place of the earlier painter's dark, carefully modeled tonalities, Rivers put his characteristically high-keyed, flickering suggestions of form. O'Hara appears, his pose taut and his presence all the more jittery because, in common with other personages on view, he has a multiple presence, like the subject of a double exposure. Whether pretending to lose himself in Géricault's precedent or stepping up the flair of his own, well-established mid-1950s style, Rivers claims an exemplary tenuousness. Yet he always makes it clear that he is the sole possessor of his seeming lack of self-possession.

Painters of the 1950s elaborated ambiguous selves in defiance of the monolithic presences of those painters who, as O'Hara put it, set aside recognizable things to pursue "the great, beautiful and solitary aim of abstract painting."[13] Pollock, Clyfford Still and other members of the New York School's first generation devised the heroic fiction of the "solitary" abstractionist. No painter can be as independent of history and colleagues as they claim to be. Nor could an artist with an entirely ambiguous being, a self without borders, have survived amid the quick-tempo sophistication of O'Hara's fifties. Like the soaring eagle of abstraction, the artist as city mouse at risk from the subtlety of his own mimesis was a carefully tended fiction.

The sharp likeness in Fairfield Porter's *Larry Rivers* (1951) also reads as a play of light, as if Porter were not so much a portraitist facing a subject as a disembodied eye seeking a purchase, however faint, on the world of specific detail. Porter never ran the risk of losing himself in pictorial delicacy, yet Frank O'Hara's "Porter Paints a Picture" implies that he did. The poet begins his essay by remarking that the painter

> lives in Southampton, Long Island, a town which . . . rather reminds you of Henry James. . . . Porter's rambling white house . . . is Jamesian, too: its many rooms invite and impose privacy to a degree; and the soft light, result of elms far and high enough to subdue the sun without really shading the house, lends subtlety to faded walls held in place by Japanese prints, Audubon birds and early de Koonings.[14]

Scanned, this passage straightforwardly sets a scene. A slower look reveals conflicts. In Fairfield Porter's house, it is difficult to distinguish invitations from impositions. The house feels big, presumably sturdy, yet the walls are faded and in some way so flimsy that they must be held in place by works of art, like interior walls in Porter's paintings. Here, existence depends on nuance. As this Jamesian house exists only in the poet's description, so Porter's paintings quietly argue that people— including presumably, himself—have their significant being only on sufferance from his brush.

When Porter wrote about Larry Rivers, a virtuoso performer in the drama of the urban self, he began by noting that Rivers first appeared "as a saxophone player, a jazz musician." Then

> his histrionic nature led him to painting when he met painters. The same trait, plus a special ability with words, a unique idiomatic carelessness of expression, made him write poetry. Finally he has taken to sculpture. If it is like an actor not to know who he is, then, like an actor, and because he likes to experiment, Rivers acts out his life in search for a sound basis. It is as if all events in which he participates were crucial moments in his autobiography.[15]

Mingling accurate reportage with plausible speculation, this passage offers a recognizable image of Larry Rivers. But, ever so faintly, it also serves as a mirror for Fairfield Porter. He, too, acted out his life as he went. A Midwesterner, Porter played the part of an esthetically inclined scion of the New

England gentry. In balanced contrast stood Rivers, a native of the Bronx in the role of Manhattan hipster.

Because Porter argued that Vuillard is a more significant artist than Cézanne, he felt compelled to oppose such Cézannian developments as cubism—even Willem de Kooning's late variations. On the other hand, Porter's friendship with action painters, figurative and not, required him to find some way to admire de Kooning, the arch action painter. His path to admiration was as twisted as the labyrinthine sensibilities of Frank O'Hara's fifties could have wished. Reviewing a group of Woman paintings exhibited in 1955, Porter recalled that in the 1940s de Kooning's art had suggested a devotion to Ingres. Then he pointed to textures in de Kooning's later works reminiscent of Delacroix, the champion of color who is traditionally seen as the opponent of Ingres's linear style. In summary, Porter argued that the paintings under review offer a "paradox": de Kooning "seems to have gotten from Ingres an appreciation of color, and it is as if Delacroix's influence led him to demonstrate Ingres's dictum that 'what is well drawn is well enough painted.'"[16] Porter invented a Porteresque de Kooning to whom he attributed the invention of de Kooningesque versions of Ingres and Delacroix. However this tactic illuminates—or obscures—de Kooning's paintings of the mid-fifties, it makes them a bank of mirrors reflecting Porter's sensibility.

Porter the critic invents a bit of himself by inventing his own Larry Rivers and de Kooning, as Porter the portraitist devises self-images by painting family and friends, objects and places. Moreover, he attributes this roundabout method of self-creation to artists he finds sympathetic. In a 1958 review, Porter said that the "breadth" of Larry Rivers's new painting and sculpture

> comes from a selection of whatever subject before you catches the attention: light on the floor, a sense of height above the street, of the street always there and alive below the window, symbols of the life in his flat, the time of day or night, the kind of day. . . . His awareness integrates, so that, as in some Symbolist poetry and some Vuillards, the only person there is the artist: the subject is fragmented.[17]

Or we read in a scattered subject a reflection of the artist's unifying will and this makes it whole.

Earlier in 1958, Grace Hartigan contributed to an *Art News* symposium called "Artists With or Against the Past." Gathered by Fairfield Porter, her statement recalls that she worked her way through abstract expressionism's "rejection of the past," then turned to the art of historical figures like Rubens, Titian, Tiepolo, Velazquez, Zurbarán, and Goya. Picasso and Matisse led her back to Pollock and de Kooning, whose paintings she now saw as laden with history and full of clues to a figurative kind of action painting. Now, she goes on,

> I can't think of anybody. Anything can be of help and finally there is no place to look outside yourself. Finally the paintings carry the story of what you have done. . . . I have talked too much and thought too much and it seems not to be the point. . . . My painting is a visual equivalent of a world of my own that I am going deeper and deeper into.[18]

In recording and editing these remarks, Porter must have given them at least a tinge of fiction. Restrained or sweeping, it was a sympathetic transformation, so one can read Hartigan's comments on her art both as documentary evidence and as an oblique reflection of Porter's esthetics of self-invention.

Frank O'Hara wrote a poem to Hartigan, "Portrait of Grace," and she is a leading candidate for the nylon-wearing other addressed by "Favorite Painting in the Metropolitan." Her *Art News* statement shows the sensibility she shared with the poet coming to the end of its frazzled rope and finding at that extremity not a dead end but a glimpse of figurative action painting's strength. In desperation Hartigan concludes that "there is no place to look outside yourself." Having accepted that, she sees her art opening onto "a world of her own." In that world, she can make anything a self-reflection. As Porter put it, "the only person there is the artist." Yet the artist's figurative impulses ensure that, again in Porter's words, art makes "the connection between yourself and everything"—or, it connects self and other in ways that give them a near but not absolute identity. The ideal was a modified solipsism.

In his contribution to the *Art News* symposium on the uses of history, Robert Goodnough said:

> The way I understand the question of representationalism is that an object does not exist as such in art but rather as

a part of an experience you have *with the object* . . . the "figure" does not exist independently but as part of the whole surface. The modern attitude toward the object is, I think, that in itself it's nothing; it's only the emblem of an experience.[19]

Again, "the only person there is the artist." During the 1950s Goodnough immersed his figures in an alloverness learned from Pollock and given order–or an orderly atmosphere–by a version of Cézanne's pictorial architecture. Combining the latter's composition with the former's anticomposition, Goodnough made himself master of an immense range of formal possibilities. Within the borders of his art, he holds absolute sway. Goodnough's signatory flourishes of paint seem to absorb his art in its own textures. Yet his "slipping glimpse" encourages us to read images of cowboys or dinosaurs or antique statuary in his painterly handwriting, and this deflects the risk of complete self-absorption. Like other figurative painters of the fifties, Goodnough could shade an effect of absence with his own presence,[20] making it difficult to know exactly how his intentions inhabit his art. At first glance, his paintings are identifiably his, yet it is never clear what he wants us to identify in his characteristic images–him, others, himself in them, others as symbols of Goodnough? The painter who throws his presence into doubt can mold that presence as he would a work of art; or, to tighten the argument to a paradox, he can achieve esthetic control of his identity by rendering it elusive on terms recognizably his own. But for the drama of self-invention to escape solipsism and achieve full scale, difficulties could not all be personal. The plot required a publicly recognized villain, a figure of authority opposed to the very notion of figurative art. Several stood ready to hand.

Thomas B. Hess, the editor who made *Art News* the journal of record for O'Hara's art world, noted in 1968 that "Clement Greenberg had once told de Kooning, 'It is impossible today to paint a face,' to which de Kooning replied, 'That's right, and it's impossible not to.'"[21] Fairfield Porter claimed to have inspired the exchange by bringing Greenberg and de Kooning together soon after the painter exhibited the first of his Woman series. When the critic announced that "You can't paint figuratively today," Porter thought to himself, "If that's what he says . . . I will do exactly what he says I can't do. That's all I will do." He "might have become an abstract painter except for that."[22] If

history's impersonal forces demanded abstraction, he would write a personal history–the chronicle of a personality–with portraits, still lifes, and landscapes. Porter worked relentlessly to suggest the transience of sunlight and shadow, yet there is a deeper reason for the instability of his pictures: with only slight modifications they would become the abstractions he said he would have painted if Greenberg hadn't forbidden it. As O'Hara wrote, it may be only Porter's "insistence on presenting differences within the compositional perception"–that is, his insistence on marking off large compositional elements with smallish representational details–"which keeps his paintings from becoming abstractions and therefore facts, in the sense that a Mondrian is a fact."[23] Larry Rivers took contrariness a step farther. Not only did he paint the figure; with *George Washington Crossing the Delaware* (1953), he satisfied his wish "to do something no one in the New York art world could doubt was *disgusting, dead,* and *absurd.*"[24]

Elaine de Kooning found an antifigurative *bête noir* in Ad Reinhardt, who wrote in 1957 that art must have "No object, no subject, no matter. No symbols, images or signs. Neither pleasure or pain."[25] De Kooning replied with "Pure Paints a Picture," a report on a visit to the studio of an imaginary abstractionist named Adolf M. Pure. Assuming the role of selfless epigone, she recorded a barrage of *obiter dicta*, all variations on Reinhardt's pronouncements. The fictive Mr. Pure believes that "the only way to arrive at Correct, Pure or Fine Art is by a series of rejections." Above all,

> There are three . . . important *No*'s to be mastered: no image, no scrimmage, and last but not least, no subject matter. However, one high-strung spectator, peering into the darkness of Pure's canvases, claims to have discovered the subject–a graveyard at night. This is erroneous. "Art can be corrected but, alas," Pure sighs, "the public cannot."[26]

First-generation New York school painters like Ad Reinhardt may not have achieved purity (whatever that might be), but they did take out a patent on the idea. It was theirs, until minimalism appeared with a new definition of pure art. For the denizens of Frank O'Hara's art world, to aspire to the absolutist ideals of Reinhardt, Newman and Rothko would have been death–or life in Mr. Pure's graveyard.[27] The younger New Yorkers came alive by sullying abstraction with references to the figure, then blurring their figures' identities—and their own. As Larry Rivers was jazz musician, painter, sculptor and poet, so Fairfield Porter was poet, critic and painter. Elaine de Kooning propagandized for the painterly figure in the pages of *Art News* when she wasn't objecting to so-called pure painting or producing painterly figures of her own. A poet, critic, and curator, Frank O'Hara made conflicts of interest a way of life.[28] For the second generation, to oppose first-generation purities with distinctive impurities was to assert one's integrity.

Mark Rothko's and Clyfford Still's presence at the California School of Fine Arts, in San Francisco, inspired a Bay Area variant of abstract expressionism. Goaded only at long distance by the exemplary anxieties of de Kooning and Pollock, California's abstract expressionists—among them David Park and Richard Diebenkorn—aspired to a monumental quietism. In 1950 Park showed a canvas called *Kids on Bikes*. Bringing one bike rider forward in cropped close-up and scattering the jagged forms of the others throughout the depths, this painting looks like a pattern of Clyfford Still's hot color made over as a quasi-realist genre scene. Diebenkorn recalls asking, "My God! What's happened to David?"[29] Soon he too was painting recognizable figures. A third convert, Elmer Bischoff, later recalled that in the early 1950s, abstract expressionism

> was playing itself dry. There was a definite cooling off. . . .
> When I was in the real grip of Abstract Expressionism,
> the marks and gestures had a hyper existence. But it was
> your own passion that inflamed those things, and there
> was just a gradual loss of passion.[30]

In New York, artists' struggles with critics, curators, and the marketplace lent strength to the personal passions that sustain abstract painting. The same mix of public struggle and private devotion impelled certain painters not only to depict figures but to insist that figures must be depicted. The Bay Area generated little of the conflict that inspires intransigence. When a painter's interest in abstract art faded, he slid with ease into figure painting, and out of it just as easily. In the early 1970s, Bischoff took up abstract painting once more, finding that recognizable motifs no longer generated the "dynamic interaction" he required.[31] Diebenkorn returned to abstraction a decade before Bischoff did. Park remained a figure painter until his death in 1960.

Bay Area painters of the 1950s, abstract and figurative, built solid compositions from color laid on in wide, textured swaths. Though Bischoff's atmospheric hues are different from, say, Park's denser ones, both persuaded gestural spontaneity to make its peace with a solidly architectural sense of order. As Bischoff sought the harmonies that would produce a "unity of feeling,"[32] Park tried to bring a painting to the point where its "vibration and rhythm . . . corresponds to the vibration and rhythm of the person" being painted.[33] Placing wide sweeps of paint on the canvas as if they were rafters in a well-made house (and reinforcing the sturdiness of his compositions when that is what his brushstrokes depict), he removed the tension between figurative and nonfigurative readings. Similarly, Bischoff eased the distinction between picturing individuals and deploying formal generalities. He has said that he "never did figurative painting where the personages were identified," preferring to give the figure the "universality" he saw as a characteristic of abstraction.[34] Bay Area figure painters smoothed over difficulties that their counterparts in New York worked hard to exaggerate.

Ignoring the common-sense assumption that friction generates unpleasantness, the poets and painters in O'Hara's art world deployed contradictory gestures in the service of a higher diplomacy—good manners in a realm of paradox. Yet diplomacy in the usual sense was not always lacking. Reviewing George McNeil's 1957 exhibition in Manhattan, James Schuyler wrote:

> Since last fall, McNeil has been painter-in-residence at
> the University of California, Berkeley. East is East, West
> is West, ever the twain shall meet: *Risorgimento*, pale as
> a flight at dawn, fast as the speed [of] an Easterner's
> dream of that far coast, an uncensored action painting.[35]

McNeil is an ecumenical figure painter, but not in the way Schuyler suggests, for the geography of his style locates New York in the West, and his dreams turn not toward California's Far West but eastward, toward Europe. In particular, the screeching color and grotesque whimsicality of his figures make him an American ally of the COBRA painters. So far as I know, the 1950s produced no entente, cordial or not, between the figurative painters of the East and West Coasts. Neither group could threaten the other, nor offer it guidance. Contact would have been pointless.

West Coast figure painting of the 1950s proposes the artist as a magnetic presence with the calm authority to define conflicts and resolve them. The ideal self of the Bay Area painter felt at home in the studio conceived as the site of an esthetic pastoral, a place at once private and open to all the transcendent currents of art and its history. Never at home, the New Yorker preferred the antipastoral of the city, where selfhood's crisis at least enjoyed the glamor of an audience. O'Hara's art world was a round of settings fit for public gestures—galleries, museums, streets in certain neighborhoods. Cornered in the studio, the New York self would strike an attitude calculated to turn this private setting into a public stage.

These East and West Coast selves look like polar opposites until we bring Chicago's figurative artists of the 1950s onto the scene. A New Yorker like Larry Rivers and a Bay Area painter like Richard Diebenkorn accepted the Renaissance and its consequences. The Chicagoan Leon Golub rejected mainstream Western tradition in favor of late, debased Hellenistic statuary, Northwestern Indian carvings, art brut, the art of the insane, and so on. Moreover, his violent—and violently eccentric—images encourage us to see ourselves and our fellows "as having undergone a holocaust or facing annihilation or mutation."[36] In the following decade, Chicago's figurative painters banded together under labels like The Hairy Who to cultivate the private obsessions of a local surrealism, grisly and whimsical by turns. During the fifties, Chicagoans used figures to address public matters. Seymour Rosofsky adapted Goya's late style to a vision of contemporary horror. The often finicky devices of Dada collage and the surrealist object took on hulking scale in George Cohen's work. H.C. Westermann charged the look of outsider art with sometimes brutal social comment. To outward appearances, at any rate, the Bay Area artists formed a small and quietly friendly community. Though rife with centrifugal forces, the New Yorkers' world cohered, thanks to a noisy, sometimes strident brand of friendship. Despite their "Monster School" tag, the Chicagoans of the 1950s never coalesced into a group.[37] For all its incompatibility, their art shared one purpose: to announce the artist's alienation in terms clear enough to be widely understood. Rather than posit an ideal self, their figurative images try to uncover what these artists saw as the actual state of the contemporary individual—terrified, wounded, and in desperate need of healing. The most suitable habitat for this image of the self was neither the artist's studio nor the art gallery, but the junk heaps of art history and the city; or the

mental ward; or the halls of the Field Museum of Natural History, where Golub and his fellow students at Chicago's Art Institute had looked for clues to a convincing image of the human figure.

Robert Beauchamp made his New York debut with paintings of naked figures squatting, cavorting, and sometimes taking part in unexplained rites against passages of flat, quasi-abstract landscape. The women have a damp, mud-caked sexuality. Beauchamp's males are fewer and look more like baboons than human beings. Irving Sandler has suggested that the artist wanted to unveil the "aborigine" hiding in the civilized self.[38] The artist's taste for debauched pastoral tempts one to see links between him and the Chicago "Monster School." But there's no connection. A brilliant ironist, Beauchamp twisted his recollections of Gauguin's Tahiti and the German expressionists' Eden into images of remarkable delicacy. He played at primitivism, as other figure painters of the fifties played at abstraction. Beauchamp's female figures are as elegantly scrawny as high-fashion models of the period. Yet his art mixes authentically primitive feelings with an urban and at times almost arch refinement. He implies that selves are double, brutal and sophisticated, and there is a familiar doubleness in his conception of painting. Several years ago he said:

> I find myself in the middle of the road as far as abstraction versus realism is concerned. Abstraction, nonobjective painting, is a limited way to paint. . . . To paint a head means more to me than to paint a circle—a nude, more than a plane of color. But why not have your cake and eat it too? Be formally strong but open the painting to many associative possibilities.[39]

Because he is at least as close to the German expressionists as to abstract expressionists, Beauchamp shows affinities with Jan Müller. A native of Germany, Müller arrived in New York in 1941, at the age of 19, bringing with him memories of Northern European modernists and Romantics.[40] Like Larry Rivers, Müller attended Hans Hofmann's school of art. For Rivers, the school was a place to begin shaping an artist's persona; Hofmann's teaching had only a secondary interest for him.[41] The reclusive Müller, who died in 1958, appears to have paid close attention to Hofmann's ideas about pictorial form. His paintings usually erect a visual architecture sturdy enough to support an array of standing, riding, levitating figures. Gravity is absent, banished by an indifference to ordinary experience. Reviewing one of Müller's New York exhibtions, the poet John Ashbery said that the artist "brings a medieval sensibility to neo-Expressionist painting." Expressionists often reinforce the emotional heat of their brushy texures with tropical reds, oranges and yellows. Though he never proscribed those colors, Müller neglected them in favor of murky near-blacks and the ghostly whites he used for flesh tones. Passages of dark but luminous blue and green suggest stained glass windows, and in 1953-54 the patterns of his imagery grew so flat that figures vanished, leaving only a suggestion of translucent mosaics. Ashbery's review continues:

> There are a number of duplications of one of Müller's favorite themes: an encounter between a nude woman and a knight on horseback in a twilit forest that could be a scene from Tasso. His preoccupations, like anyone's, can become annoying; one is continually wondering what led him to choose this odd form of expression, and his masked figures offer no clue to what secret, if any, they have been entrusted with. Perhaps that is the very explanation of the rude, mysterious force these pictures have.[42]

Ashbery seems to be miffed by Müller's hermetic iconography. Like his friends O'Hara and Schuyler, he prefers the ambiguities generated by social exchange to those elaborated in private by a secretive vision. Using "rude" to mean primeval and coupling it with "mysterious," he offers the word as a compliment to make up for his peevishness about the artist's indecipherable "preoccupations." But the compliment sounds half-hearted, for Ashbery also means us to understand "rude" as "unmannerly." Müller rejected the high-strung protocol devised by the figurative action painters for assembling and disassembling the self and others before the spectator's eyes. The leading citizens of O'Hara's art world expected individuality to be, if not vulnerable, then at least permeable to social and pictorial currents. Like his knights on horseback, Müller is armored against slipping glimpses.

Müller's art may have looked impossibly aloof to Ashbery, yet it helped to certify the pertinence of the figure for younger New York painters like Peter Dean, Peter Passuntino and others who banded together toward the end of the 1960s in a group called

Rhino Horn. Like Müller, they treated the figure as a symbol, not as a site for the cultivation of esthetic and personal ambiguities. In the Rhino Horn orbit but never an official member of the group, Bob Thompson also learned from Müller's patterns of human form flattened against schematic landscapes. But where the older painter's palette is cold and his narratives have an elegiac feel, Thompson uses hot colors and his tableaux, while no less puzzling than Müller's, buzz with sensuality.

An accomplished athlete and, like Larry Rivers, a jazz musician, Thompson shared Rivers's belief in the futility of formal invention. After a trip to Europe and its museums, Thompson recalled that he

> began to think, God, I look at Poussin and he's got it all there. Why are all these people running around trying to be original when they should just go ahead and be themselves, and that's the originality of it all. . . . You can't draw a new form. The form has already been drawn.[43]

Historical precedent permits three responses. Awed acceptance stunts the artist. Defiance must always fail; since one cannot step outside one's culture, the attempt to reject the past leads to a dead end or in a very few cases (Clyfford Still's, for example, or Jackson Pollock's) produces major innovation. The figurative painters of the 1950s chose the third response to history. They embraced it. They drew it close to them and, to paraphrase Thompson, they grappled with forms that had already been drawn. They tried to wrest individuality from precedents, recent and distant, whose authority threatened to crush them. Moreover, they succeeded. In reinventing the figure, each of these painters devised emblems of an immediately recognizable self.

Toward the end of the decade, Thomas B. Hess cast about for a parallel to the 1950s in New York. The only comparable place was Paris, of course, but at what period? Not, Hess decided, Paris from 1907 to 1937, when manifestos drafted like declarations of war recruited artists to one or another avant-garde position. No, he said, the 1950s in New York suggested Paris in the 1860s, a time illuminated by the light that spread from the canvases of the impressionists to those of their allies, accomplices and hangers-on. There were leaders in that milieu but few artists sufficiently blinkered to want to play the part of follower. Skepticism obscured the sharp, partisan lines drawn by the occasional militant, so the politics of style and personality were lively but nebulous. Impressionism sustained an impure situation, a task action painting performed even better. "Like the Paris Manner," wrote Hess,

> the New York Manner is . . . cosmopolitan, international, intellectual and radical in approach—each picture is painted as if for the first time; the questions of doubt are never answered, but [personal] style consciously is related to [generally shared] Manner.[44]

Setting aside "questions of doubt," New York artists conspicuous in the 1960s produced an American variation on the avant-garde Paris of 1907-37. Sharply defined styles handed down decisions on the figure with a certainty that put the matter beyond appeal. Minimalism and color-field painting were against it. Pop art accepted the figure, but only in readymade form. This firmness about subject matter was the product of confidence about the nature of art. Despite the deep and sometimes bitter differences between the proponents of color-field painting, minimalism, and pop, all agreed that art realized itself by achieving progress. No more fretting about one's relationship with Velazquez or Picasso. No more cultivation of the

ambiguity that blurs images, style, and roles. In other words, no more elegant, teasing games about identity and power. To the question of who or what was in charge, mainstream sixties art had a brutally simple answer: historical necessity. Hence the major artist was the one who knew how to serve that impersonal force as a vehicle. The only argument—and it was violently disruptive—concerned the proper way to define history's demands. With the forces of historical advance at least ostensibly in charge of the nature and meaning of art, there appeared to be no reason to make a topic of the self and its vexed dealings with present and past. That topic had rendered the fifties a murky decade. Its dismissal seemed to simplify matters. A second-generation color-field painter said in 1971 that "Art is becoming neat and clean . . . unlike the art of the fifties and forties which was cloudy."[45] The obvious virtues of neatness had begun to disappear by the time this artist spoke out in their favor. By the mid-1970s, the scene had clouded up considerably. Though critics ignored them, painterly figures never entirely disappeared during these years. Then, in the early 1980s, they loomed out of the art-world cloud, the work of German, Italian, and American neo-expressionists. The self and its doubts had returned to stage center. This was a welcome change, even though the neo-expressionist figure looked less like the progeny of the figurative fifties than an unintended burlesque. ∎

Notes

1. Harold Rosenberg, "Action Painting: Crisis and Distortion," in *The Anxious Object* (Chicago and London: The University of Chicago Press, 1982), pp. 40-41.

2. In 1954 Frank O'Hara noted that "two years ago, in a talk at the Hansa Gallery, Clement Greenberg declared that abstraction was the major mode of expression in our time, that any other mode was necessarily minor; this was straight observation from the point of view of historical criticism. But a year later James Fitzsimmons, writing in *Arts and Architecture*, remarked that some of the young painters had lost heart and abandoned abstract-expressionism in a cowardly fashion to return to representational work. It is against just such an implied protocol that abstract-expressionism has always taken up a strong position." See "Nature and New Painting" (1954), in *Standing Still and Walking in New York*, ed. Donald Allen (Bolinas, California: Grey Fox Press, 1975), pp. 43-44. Elaine de Kooning took exception to these same remarks by Greenberg and Fitzsimmons in "Subject: What, How or Who?" *Art News* 54 (April 1955), pp. 26-29, pp. 61-62.

3. J[ames] S[chuyler], "Lester Johnson," *Art News* 57 (March 1958), p. 40.

4. Willem de Kooning, "Content is a Glimpse." Excerpts from an interview with David Sylvester, *Location* 1, no. 1 (Spring 1963); reprinted in Thomas B. Hess, *Willem de Kooning* (New York: The Museum of Modern Art, 1968), p. 148.

5. Harold Rosenberg reported the

phrase in "De Kooning: On the Borders of the Act" (1966), *The Anxious Object* (Chicago and London: The University of Chicago Press, 1982), p. 126. See also Hess, *Willem de Kooning*, p. 125.

6. Hess, *Willem de Kooning*, p. 100.

7. Though de Kooning pointed to "the grin of Mesopotamian idols" at the origin of his Woman paintings—see Rosenberg, "De Kooning: On the Borders of the Act," *The Anxious Object*, p. 126—he did not offer these works as invocations of premodern myth; rather, they call on ancient art, contemporary advertising, and the traditions of formal portraiture to evoke terrors inherent in contemporary sexuality.

8. J[ames] S[chuyler], "Grace Hartigan," *Art News* 58, no. 4 (May 1959), p. 13.

9. J[ames] S[chuyler], "Elaine de Kooning," *Art News* 56, no. 7 (November 1957), p. 12.

10. L[awrence] C[ampbell], "Elaine de Kooning Paints a Picture," *Art News* 59, no. 8 (December 1960), p. 62.

11. Frank O'Hara, "Larry Rivers: Why I Paint As I Do" (1956), *Art Chronicles 1954-1966* (New York: Braziller, 1975), pp. 117-18.

12. Ibid., p. 114.

13. O'Hara, "Nature and New Painting," in *Standing Still and Walking in New York*, p. 45.

14. O'Hara, "Porter Paints a Picture" (1955), in *Standing Still and Walking in New York*, p. 52.

15. Fairfield Porter, "Rivers Paints a Picture," *Art News* 52, no. 9 (January 1954), p. 57.

16. F[airfield] P[orter], "Willem de Kooning," *Art News* 54, no. 7 (November 1955), p. 49.

17. F[airfield] P[orter], "Larry Rivers," *Art News* 57, no. 8 (December 1958), p. 14.

18. F[airfield] P[orter], "Hartigan," *Art News* 57, no. 4 (Summer 1958), pp. 46, 57.

19. P[arker] T[yler], "Goodnough," *Art News* 57, no. 4 (Summer 1958), p. 43.

20. Fairfield Porter's "special gift is of catching the nuance of vacancy in a room or landscape, the unseen presences that human use and cultivation create." J[ames] S[chuyler], "Fairfield Porter," *Art News* 57, no. 3 (May 1958), p. 13.

21. Hess, *Willem de Kooning*, p. 74.

22. John Ashbery et al., *Fairfield Porter: Realist Painter in an Age of Abstraction* (Boston: Museum of Fine Arts, 1982), p. 56.

23. O'Hara, "Porter Paints a Picture," in *Standing Still and Walking in New York*, p. 55.

24. O'Hara, "Larry Rivers: Why I Paint As I Do," *Art Chronicles 1954-1966*, pp. 111-12.

25. Ad Reinhardt, "Twelve Rules for a New Academy," *Art News* 56, no. 3 (May 1957), p. 56. A summary version of the "Twelve Rules" appears in Lucy Lippard, *Ad Reinhardt* (New York: Harry N. Abrams, 1981), pp. 140-41.

26. Elaine de Kooning, "Pure Paints a Picture," *Art News* 56, no. 4 (Summer 1957), p. 57.

27. "The artists I knew at that time knew perfectly well who was Great and they weren't going to begin to imitate their works, only their spirit. When someone did a false Clyfford Still or Rothko it was talked about for weeks. They hadn't read Sartre's *Being and Nothingness* for nothing." Frank O'Hara, "Larry Rivers: A Memoir" (1965), in *Standing Still and Walking in New York*, p. 170.

28. Edward Lucie-Smith, "An Interview with Frank O'Hara" (1965), in *Standing Still and Walking in New York*, pp. 4, 6.

29. Thomas Albright, *Art in the San Francisco Bay Area: 1945-1980* (Berkeley and Los Angeles: University of California Press, 1985), p. 57.

30. Robert M. Frash, *Elmer Bischoff 1947-1985* (Laguna Beach, California: Laguna Art Museum, 1985), p. 15.

31. Henry T. Hopkins, "Is the Mainstream Flowing West?" *Art News* 81, no. 10 (January 1982), p. 75.

32. Frash, *Elmer Bischoff*, p. 15.

33. David Park, "Abstract to Realist," *Art in America* 46, no. 4 (Winter 1958-59), p. 33.

34. Ibid.

35. J[ames] S[chuyler], *Art News* 55, no. 10 (February 1957), pp. 9-10.

36. Leon Golub, in Peter Selz, *New Images of Man* (New York: The Museum of Modern Art, 1959), p. 76.

37. Paul Carroll, "Here Come the Chicago Monsters," *Chicago Perspective* (April 1964).

38. I[rving] S[andler], "Robert Beauchamp, *Art News* 58, no. 6 (October 1959), p. 58.

39. Robert Beauchamp, "Self-Interview," *Robert Beauchamp: American Expressionist* (Syracuse, New York: Everson Art Museum, 1984), p. 19.

40. Martica Sawin, "Jan Müller: 1922-1958," *Arts Magazine* 33, no. 5 (February 1959), p. 40.

41. O'Hara, "Larry Rivers: Why I Paint As I Do," *Art Chronicles 1954-1966*, p. 110.

42. J[ohn] A[shbery], "Jan Müller," *Art News* 56, no. 2 (January 1958), pp. 16-17.

43. Gylbert Coker, *Bob Thompson* (New York: The New School Art Center, 1969), p. 19.

44. Thomas B. Hess, "Younger Artists and the Unforgivable Crime," *Art News* 56, no. 2 (April 1957), pp. 48-49.

45. Simone Swan, "Conversation with Peter Bradley," *The Deluxe Show* (Houston: The Menil Foundation, 1971), p. 67.

Figuring Out the Fifties

Judith E. Stein

In 1952 the young Alex Katz was given some proscriptive advice by a well-intentioned acquaintance: "Figuration is obsolete and color is French."[1] Encoded in this admonition, which Katz did not heed, was the teleological promise that American abstract expressionism was the culminating phase of artistic progress. Abstraction had transcended depictions of the figure, and to work with representational images was to go backward.[2]

The fifties were the years of the hegemony of abstract expressionism, America's first truly international art mode. In the late 1940s, in the wake of the devastations of World War II, many first-generation New York School artists had rejected figuration as too literal a way to address human concerns. As expressionists, they chose the language of abstraction as a more spiritual alternative. But in the fifties, a younger generation of painters came to maturity impatient with the limitations of nonobjective imagery. Although they accepted as a given the gestural style and methods of action painting and courted the serendipitous process of discovery in the act of painting, they shared what poet and critic John Ashbery has termed an "'OK but let's see what else there is' attitude."[3]

As media attention focused on such mythic heroes of abstract expressionism as Jackson Pollock, Franz Kline and Willem de Kooning, a growing number of younger painters were extending the range of expressionism by exploring the expressive potential of the human form. These second and third generation New York School artists were aware of the semifigurative works of Pollock, executed between 1951 and 1953, and of de Kooning's 1950-55 Woman series. If they were not directly influenced by these departures from total abstraction, they were encouraged nonetheless by the visible exercise of esthetic freedom.

The example of older modernists then exhibiting in New York— Vaclav Vytlacil, Morris Kantor, Balcomb Greene, Nicholas Vasileff, Byron Browne, Rico Lebrun, Abraham Rattner— would have been known to them, but these young painters felt they had more in common with the abstract expressionists than with members of this earlier, cubist-influenced figurative group. To puzzle out the 1950s from the vantage point of the 1980s is to reconstruct the climate of response to figuration through contemporary commentaries, oral history, and an accounting of the major museum exhibitions of the period.

Many of the artists who employed recognizable images in the fifties were breaking an implicit taboo. Critic Lawrence Campbell, in a 1955 review of Grace Hartigan's new figurative canvases, observed that the artist was

> in revolt against the puritanism of modern artists. She does things that are simply not done in her social circle, and her motivation is a desire for freedom. She can look at the sculptural mannequins dressed like brides in the show windows of Grand Street and think how nice they would be in a painting and not feel guilty about it.[4]

That same year, in an *Art News* article on subject matter, Elaine de Kooning chided the disgruntled abstractionists who resented those artists using representation. She likened their moral indignation to that of suffragists after "they have had the vote for quite a while." For her, the baffling issue was that some even wanted "to take the vote away from the other side."[5]

The struggle to "give the vote" to abstraction had been a long one, and the American public had never been at ease with the foreign modes of the twentieth century. In the decade following the Armory Show, many American artists worked abstractly, absorbing the tenets of European modernism through study abroad or by example of those who had. But in the thirties, American scene painting held many modernists in its sway and even made converts of some of them. Thomas Hart Benton, for example, under whom Jackson Pollock studied in the early thirties, had been an abstract painter in the twenties and a decade later shifted to regionalist representations. During the war years and into the fifties, the general public was to remain highly suspicious of abstraction, considered by many as un-American. It was a rebellious sense of going against the grain, joined with their certainty of abstraction's moral superiority, that helped shape the doctrinaire stance of many nonrepresentational painters in the fifties.

The critics as well as the artists had to confront the widespread public prejudice in favor of representational art. It was as a champion of abstraction that Clement Greenberg could argue in 1954 that "the presence or absence of a recognizable image has no more to do with value in painting or sculpture than the presence or absence of a libretto has to do with value in music."[6] Regardless of the equity of this pronouncement, he was not neutral in his judgment of New York expressionists who used the figure. Grace Hartigan remembers that Greenberg told her to stop when she put aside abstraction and began working on her figurative Old Master series in 1952.[7]

While Greenberg's convictions took strength by combating the public's negative response to abstraction, others felt empowered by opposing Clement Greenberg. Fairfield Porter recounted that his regular arguments with the forceful and articulate critic partially explain why he never became an abstract painter.

> I introduced [Greenberg] to de Kooning . . . and he said to de Kooning (who was painting the women), "You can't paint this way nowadays." And I thought: Who the hell is he to say that? He said, "You can't paint figuratively today." And I thought: If that's what he says, I think I will do just exactly what he says I can't do. That's all I will do. I might have become an abstract painter except for that.[8]

Although this incident, whose veracity continues to be debated with impassioned commentary,[9] was in all likelihood not the decisive factor in Porter's commitment to the figure, a similar sense of the perceived power of Greenberg's opinions is evident in a conversation recollected by Thomas Hess:

> It is impossible today to paint a face, pontificated the critic Clement Greenberg around 1950. "That's right," said de Kooning, "and it's impossible not to."[10]

Robert Goodnough recalls a phone conversation in the early sixties in which he revealed to Greenberg, "I have this conflict between the abstract and the figurative," to which Greenberg replied: "I don't think there's any conflict." Goodnough never pressed him for a further explanation, assuming rightly or wrongly that Greenberg would have discouraged his figurative work.[11]

Many artists of an older generation who had made an earlier commitment to representational art felt beleaguered in the fifties as the art world media focused more and more on abstractionists. *Reality, A Journal of Artists' Opinions* sprang up in New York in the winter of 1953 "to rise to the defense of any painter's right to paint any way he wants."[12] The editorial committee, which included such well-known realist artists as Isabel Bishop, Edward Hopper, Jack Levine, Raphael Soyer, and Henry Varnum Poor, maintained that "unlike *Art News*, we

want to suppress no way of painting."[13] *Reality* published a letters forum in which Rudolf Baranik could write that "there is nothing basically inhuman, fanatical, depraved or mystic about nonobjective painting or sculpture,"[14] while reactionary voices could characterize action painters as "play[ing] with [their] tools in unfruitful ejaculations of non-art" or rail against "the ritualistic double talk of the cult of the doodle, and the elevation of the Accidental School of painting."[15]

By the late fifties it was clear even to Philip Pavia, the partisan publisher of *It is*, a magazine of abstract art, that the nonabstract artist was being neglected in the New York-based art press. In an open letter to Leslie Katz, the new publisher of *Arts Magazine*, Pavia admitted being forced "into an unorthodox position; I am begging you to give the *representational* artist a better deal. The neglected representational and near-abstract artists, not the abstractionists, need a champion these days."[16] Significantly, many of the artists themselves wrote articles and reviews, for example, Robert Goodnough, Elaine de Kooning, and Fairfield Porter. Although the figurative expressionists lacked advocates of the stature of Clement Greenberg or Harold Rosenberg, they were taken up by a receptive group of critics who either defined abstract expressionism to include them or set them outside of it as the new radicals. In a 1959 discussion of the achievements of Jan Müller, who had recently died, Martica Sawin noted that Müller and his Hansa Gallery colleagues, all former students of Hans Hofmann,[17] were "representatives of a new generation to whom figurative art was in a sense more revolutionary than abstraction."[18]

Poet, critic and curator Frank O'Hara was one of several key individuals who facilitated the acceptance of the new figuration. Because his support of New York School abstraction was never in question, his contagious enthusiasm for such figurative artists as Grace Hartigan, Larry Rivers, and Alex Katz was persuasive. In his poetry, he celebrated the process and content of Rivers's and Hartigan's paintings.[19] As a critic, he wrote "Nature and New Painting" in 1954, an elegant defense of those young painters, namely Hartigan, Rivers, Elaine de Kooning, Jane Freilicher, Robert de Niro, Felix Pasilis and Wolf Kahn, who responded to "the siren-like call of nature."[20] Here O'Hara rejected the notion, put forth by critic James Fitzsimmons the previous year, "that some of the young painters had lost heart

Hans Hofmann
Scintillating Space, 1954
oil on canvas
84⅛ x 43⅜ inches
Collection University Art Museum,
University of California, Berkeley; gift of
the artist (1966.47)

and abandoned Abstract Expressionism in cowardly fashion to return to representational work."

O'Hara was also reacting to Clement Greenberg, who in a 1952 talk at the Hansa Gallery, had declared that "abstraction was the major mode of expression in our time; [and] that any other mode was necessarily minor." Noting that these new representational artists "have no group . . . mail no manifestos and . . . do not favor a given look or an external content," O'Hara declared them against only an "implied protocol." In their revolt against academicism, he aligned them *within* abstract expressionism, which had always taken a strong position against an implied protocol, "whether at the Metropolitan Museum or the Artists Club." This refusal to place those he supported outside of the tradition of abstract expressionism would be echoed in 1960 by Thomas Hess, who wrote that "the 'new figurative painting' which some have been expecting as a reaction against Abstract Expressionism was implicit in it at the start, and is one of its most lineal continuities."[21]

One of the nation's most respected art critics in the fifties, Tom Hess was the author of *Abstract Painting: Background and American Phase*. Published in 1951, it was the first significant book on abstract painting in New York. Hess was to extend a crucial critical boost to figurative expressionism when, for the Stable Gallery's 1955 *U.S. Painting: Some Recent Directions*, he identified twenty-three important painters pursuing new directions, the majority of whom were using representational images. His sampling, featured again in the 1956 *Art News Annual*, included Wolf Kahn, Nell Blaine, Fairfield Porter, Larry Rivers, Elaine de Kooning and Robert Goodnough, who was then working nonfiguratively. Hess identified five major influences affecting these younger artists, citing the example of first-generation abstract expressionists with illustrations of a recent large-scale Franz Kline, one of de Kooning's Women, a semifigurative Jackson Pollock of the early fifties, as well as the "ideas and pictures" of such master teachers as Clyfford Still and Hans Hofmann.[22]

Hans Hofmann was a seminal figure for the majority of nonabstract expressionist New York artists in the fifties. For example, George McNeil studied with him in the thirties, Larry Rivers in the late forties, and Robert Goodnough, Robert

Vaclav Vytlacil
Figures of Pompeii, 1951
oil on canvas, mounted on board
72⅜ x 56¼ inches
Collection The Pennsylvania Academy of
the Fine Arts, Joseph E. Temple Fund

Bob Thompson at El Cosorio Gallery,
Ibiza, Spain, 1963

Beauchamp and Jan Müller in the early fifties. Müller was
directed to Hofmann by Vaclav Vytlacil, his earlier teacher at
the Art Students League, who had been one of Hofmann's first
American students in 1921.[23] Lester Johnson had studied with
Alexander Masley and Cameron Booth, who like Vytlacil, had
both journeyed to Europe to work under Hofmann in the late
twenties and early thirties. While never a student of Hofmann's,
Grace Hartigan was exposed to his esthetic philosophy by serv-
ing as a model in his classes at one point in her early career.[24]
Elaine de Kooning sat in on some of his Provincetown classes
and subsequently wrote a major article on him,[25] and Bob
Thompson had been a close associate of several former Hofmann students, notably Jan Müller.

Hofmann's teaching method centered around drawing from the
model or still life.[26] Wolf Kahn has captured the unique quality
of Hofmann's genius as an instructor:

> He taught like the Bible teacher — a man of contradictions
> when taken at his word, but clear and profound when
> taken as a whole. He was useful in two ways, first, to
> follow, then, to rebel against. But when I rebelled I was
> aware that it was Hofmann himself who had given me the
> weapon for it.[27]

Tom Hess observed that even as Hofmann taught modernist
theory he provided his students with the means to depart from
it. As Hess noted, although Hofmann's students were urged to
use spontaneity in rearranging and reassembling the literal data
before him, the model remained

> a touchstone with which he never must lose contact. . . .
> So it is not surprising that many of Hofmann's students,
> reacting from his insistence on a right kind of modern
> painting, took the simple step to a closer identification of
> the picture with the still life, model or landscape. It is
> almost as if Hofmann had planned such an escape hatch
> from his system.[28]

Nonetheless, some of his students chafed under his doctrinaire
approach. Hofmann didn't encourage close representation:
"Objective renderings are too often minimized: the human
figure becomes a doll; a landscape, [becomes] a marionette
set," he told Elaine de Kooning in 1949 in an interview for *Art
News*.[29] Eight years later Hofmann would discourage the
figurative canvases of his short-term student Red Grooms,
whose images he critiqued as representing "little dolls."[30]

Yet Hofmann was supportive of the figurative efforts of some of his students. John Bernard Myers related the following story about Larry Rivers: "One day he brought Mr. Hofmann an oil on canvas; it was abstract. 'Larry,' [Hofmann] said, 'who told you to paint that? You'll never be an abstract artist; stick to what you do best.'"[31] According to Rivers, after a year of seeing his fellow students render the nude solely in abstract terms, "I became frantic to draw the figure, and no more advanced than Corot."[32]

Hofmann maintained many warm friendships with his students, and with his fellow German-born pupil Jan Müller the bond was particularly strong. The painter Dody Müller, Jan's widow, describes a telling incident between the two artists whose mutual respect and affection was similar to that of father and son. She recalls that at Müller's opening at Provincetown's Sun Gallery during the summer of 1956, the two men became embroiled in a heated argument regarding Jan's change from abstraction to figuration. Neither man would concede to the other's views, but the next morning Hofmann delivered Müller a conciliatory note which tacitly acknowledged that "there's no harm in figuration."[33] Although early in the fifties Müller had worked both figuratively and in a mosaic-like abstract style that was close to a mode of Hofmann's, he had made an abrupt shift to total figuration following his heart operation in 1954. In explaining the alteration in his approach to painting, Müller once remarked, "Abstraction is no longer enough for me. So I'm returning to the image. The image gives one a wider sense of communication."[34]

For Müller, figuration widened his ability to convey his content based on literary and mythological themes. The expansion of expressive content was likewise the motivation for the emergence of the figure in the work of Robert Beauchamp and Lester Johnson. Beauchamp, who had been working with the figure since 1953, told a *Time* magazine reporter in 1962: "It was an emotional thing. I felt abstract art was too remote from immediate life, that I had to wear blinders when I walked out onto the street."[35] Although the laconic Beauchamp may not have said so at the time, figuration gave him access to the imagery of his fantasies and dreams, as well as to the stylistic traditions of art history. In a published conversation about an exhibition of Beauchamp's work, the painters Lois Dodd, Sally Hazelet and Philip Pearlstein remarked, "When you first come

in it's all Beauchamp, then you begin to discover the subject matter, then you see the influences . . . Picasso, Degas, Gauguin, Japanese, Klimt, Schiele, de Kooning, Mantegna, Egyptian art. But it's all Beauchamp."[36]

Lester Johnson turned to expressionist figuration to extend the emotional range and content of abstract expressionism. After passing through an early exploration of pure form, Johnson's art in the fifties, whether abstract or figurative, had taken as its subject the human condition. But his style and scale were to change in response to action painting:

> I gradually got involved with what Rosenberg calls the arena, which is quite different than European easel painting. I got very much into active painting. . . . My only problem was that I thought it very quickly became a cliché . . . and I thought the way to go would be the figure. It seemed to me so obvious that you had to frustrate [pure action painting]—it was too easy, they could make the drips, the gestures—it was so beautiful and everybody loved them but they were empty. I was into human content so I used it, and I found it a very, very exciting thing to do. I did a lot of paintings at the time where you can hardly see the figure, but it's there, it's all mixed up but it's always there, the position, where it is and what it's doing.[37]

By the second half of the fifties, Lester Johnson's unique mixture of figural subjects, urban content and expressionist style exerted a significant influence on the younger generation of New York and Provincetown artists, who listened appreciatively to his public presentations at The Club and who regarded him as one of the most inspiring figurative expressionists then working.[38] He was "an intellectual signpost," according to his contemporary Sidney Geist, who remembers an occasion when Johnson, speaking on a panel at The Club, "said something so beautiful that you could feel in the air that everybody was touched."[39]

His example was especially important for the former Hofmann students associated with the Sun Gallery in Provincetown.[40] Under the directorship of painter Yvonne Andersen and poet Val Falcone, the Sun held a series of weekly exhibitions each summer from 1955 through 1959. The Sun's network of figurative artists included Mary Frank, Robert Frank, Red

Grooms, Allan Kaprow, Alex Katz, Marcia Marcus, Jay Milder, Dody Müller, Jan Müller, Lucas Samaras, Bob Thompson, Tony Vevers, and Robert Whitman. Johnson's expressionist figuration was a potent vehicle for his interest in the urban experience, a concern shared by many of those involved with the gallery, which mounted two group exhibitions on the subject of the city in 1958.[41] During the winter of 1958-59, Red Grooms and Jay Milder opened an innovative alternative space, the City Gallery, in Red's lower Manhattan loft. Lester Johnson taught painting classes there and was an exhibitor, along with Claes Oldenburg, Jim Dine, Mimi Gross, Bob Thompson and Alex Katz.

Several of the Sun Gallery artists were also associated with the cooperative Hansa Gallery in New York. Artists from both galleries embodied in their art and in their attitudes an impatience with abstraction and an involvement with the working methods of action painting. Sculptor George Segal, who in the fifties exhibited figurative expressionist canvases as a member of the Hansa group, has reflected on these times, speaking for himself and for his Hansa colleague Allan Kaprow:

> We found it rather amazing that so much avant-garde, 20th-century art was rooted in physical experience of the real world and suddenly the Abstract Expressionists were legislating any reference to the physical world totally out of art. This was outrageous to us.[42]

Kaprow's concern for a concrete art and his interest in the physical process of gestural expressionism led him to develop the art form known as "happenings," which were live art events enacted by the artist and his friends.

This literally figural genre emphasizing the "act" in action painting attracted the involvement of several artists affiliated with the Sun Gallery, where one of the first happenings, Red Grooms's *Play Called Fire*, was staged in the summer of 1958. At the opening of the Reuben Gallery in the fall of 1959, Lester Johnson took part in Allan Kaprow's 90 minute *18 Happenings in Six Parts* in New York, in which he and Alfred Leslie were assigned the task of responsively painting strokes on either side of a canvas.[43]

Parodic humor was another manifestation of the links between figurative expressionism and the happenings: Claes Oldenburg, in one of his own early happenings, used a group of writhing, primeval figures that Robert Beauchamp interpreted as a clear takeoff on the painted bodies involved in mysterious ceremonies which Beauchamp himself depicted in the late fifties and early sixties.[44]

If Hans Hofmann's teaching methodology provided the young painters of the fifties with the tools to approach the figure, then the examples of Jackson Pollock and Willem de Kooning supplied them with iconoclastic role models unafraid of breaking what Frank O'Hara had termed the "implied protocol" of abstraction. Throughout most of his career, Pollock worked with the imagery of his unconscious, choosing either to veil the resulting figures or to expose them, as he did in the black-and-white paintings of 1951-53.[45] He was uncomfortable with the label of abstract expressionism:

> I don't care for "abstract expressionism" . . . and it's certainly not "nonobjective," and not "nonrepresentational" either. I'm very representational some of the time, and a little all of the time. But when you're painting out of your unconscious, figures are bound to emerge.[46]

Pollock's example was important to Jan Müller, who felt he could never have painted the way he did had it not been for the example of Pollock's "grandeur."[47] To Robert Goodnough, who wrote the 1951 *Art News* article "Jackson Pollock Paints a Picture," the most impressive aspect of Pollock was "the freedom with which he approached what he was doing."[48]

Willem de Kooning also refused to adhere to any modernist rules of purity that would restrict his painterly options. When, after a period of abstract painting in the mid- to late-forties, de Kooning returned to his earlier theme of women, he jolted the New York art world, which had come to regard him as having transcended figuration. Dody Müller recalls being stopped on the street in the early fifties by acquaintances eager to share the startling news that de Kooning was painting the figure.[49] In his 1956 *Art News Annual* piece on recent painting trends, Tom Hess cited de Kooning's Women as the one example of recent art most appreciated by the majority of the young painters under discussion.[50] The Woman series, referred to as the "symbol for the opposition" in a 1962 *Art News* article on recent figurative painting,[51] was "the image of the figure in the 1950s most acceptable to the avant-garde," as Philip Pearlstein disapprovingly noted in a companion essay.[52]

It was the content and the form of de Kooning's women that seemed to touch some elemental nerve in its audience. Contemporary commentators reached into prehistory and pop culture to describe them. In 1955 Leo Steinberg wrote that the Women were "disastrously erotic in some remote, paleolithic way";[53] Tom Hess that same year characterized one as "like a Michelangelo sibyl who has read Moon Mullins and is turning into a landscape";[54] and Manny Farber in 1959 portrayed another as a "Sadie Thompson-ish tootsie caught in a maelstrom."[55]

Like much of the figurative work influenced by de Kooning's example, the Woman series had more in common with abstract expressionism than it did with the enduring figurative tradition in American art. Fairfield Porter, who acknowledged a debt to de Kooning's work, as he did to the paintings of his contemporaries Larry Rivers, Jane Freilicher, Alex Katz, and John Button, said, "I feel more at home with [the abstract expressionists] than I do with people who aggressively call themselves realists."[56] For his part, Porter, for whom the process of painting was an act of discovery, felt that there was no hierarchical distinction bewteen abstract and figurative art.[57]

For Elaine de Kooning, who recognizes Willem de Kooning and Arshile Gorky as her major role models, the ability to switch off between abstraction and figuration was something she accepted without question. She instinctively distrusted modernist ideologues who ranked one approach above another. Already noted for her deft drawing skills, she began studying with de Kooning when she was eighteen. From the time of her earliest work, which was "mostly figurative, but from a very abstract vantage point," her method reflected the attitude that "there's just as much variety possible painting figuratively as there is abstractly."[58] After a summer of painting abstractions at Black Mountain College in 1948, she returned to the figure, beginning with a series of drawings and paintings of seated men and later expanding to images of athletes in motion.

The way Elaine de Kooning approached her fifties paintings of identifiable subjects revealed her commitment to the strategies of abstract expressionism. In a statement published in a 1959 issue of *It is*, she expressed herself as an action painter:

> A painting to me is primarily a verb, not a noun—an event first and only secondarily an image. . . . I want

more than composition in painting. For one thing, I want *gesture*. . . . I see everything as possessing or possessed by gesture. I've often thought of my paintings as having an axis around which everything revolves. . . . When I painted my seated men, I saw them as gyroscopes. Portraiture has always fascinated me because I love the particular gesture of a particular expression or stance. . . . Working on the figure, I wanted paint to sweep through as feelings sweep through. Then I wanted the paint to sweep the figure along with it—and got involved with men in action—abstract action, action for its own sake—the game. And finally I wanted the paint to sweep through, around, over and past, to hack away at contours and engulf silhouettes.[59]

So broad was the definition of New York School expressionism, which connoted mural scale as well as passionate process, that painters as divergent in style as Elaine de Kooning and Alex Katz could fit within its context. In the early sixties, Alex Katz responded to a questionnaire regarding his ambition as a painter by writing that he wished "to continue the great tradition of the New York School."[60]

During the fifties, the art press often linked Larry Rivers with the abstract expressionists. This puzzled and irritated Selden Rodman, who went to interview Rivers in 1956 for his book *Conversations with Artists*. Rodman was hostile to New York School abstraction, favoring such representational expressionists as Rico Lebrun and Leonard Baskin. In advance of meeting Rivers, he conjectured unsympathetically that the editors of *Art News* recognized "the abstract expressionist's compulsion to dehumanize" in the "cold detachment" of Rivers's figurative paintings.[61] When the question of commonalities was finally put to the artist, Rivers observed: "the abstract expressionists are interested in what happens accidentally on the canvas, and so am I; that's somewhat the same kick, isn't it?"[62] Rivers went on to explain that he felt "related and unrelated" to Pollock and de Kooning, who were of a different generation.

Rivers's figure paintings of the fifties were to go through several distinct phases. They evolved from the raw, emotionally charged paintings of de Kooningesque women, through the somber Old Masterish larger-than-life studies of the single nude, past the more lyrical coloration and realistic depictions of

his mother-in-law, to a series of brushy, fragmented, near-abstract figural renderings. Because his human subjects were primarily a vehicle for an ever changing content, he was not interested in aligning himself with doctrinaire representationalists. Rivers recalls being contacted by one of his fellow classmates at Hofmann's studio, Seymour Remenick, who had painted abstractions in the forties and had switched to representational images "because Hofmann made me see what's in nature."[63] It was the early fifties,

when the abstract thing inundated the art world and gave such a low place to the figure. [Remenick] asked if I wanted to join a group that was adamantly figurative, and I wouldn't do it. I thought that they were corny. They took themselves seriously in a way that didn't allow for a certain kind of experimentation. While I used the figure, I had some other idea what it meant. . . . I used it to the glory of something about surface and plastic qualities. . . . At that time I thought that to think that a figure was a morally superior thing to be involved with was somehow almost not nice. I felt as if [their stand] was built on jealousy a great deal. They just didn't like the laurels that were being pinned on [the abstract] painters.[64]

Larry Rivers's figure paintings may well have been the most controversial ones of the decade. In 1961 Rivers described that, in the early fifties, he had been "cocky and angry enough at the time to want to do something no one in the New York art world doubted was disgusting, dead and absurd."[65] When his 1954 large nude portrait *Augusta* was shown at the 1955 Whitney Annual, Lawrence Campbell approvingly noted the freshness of "its unabashed, unidealized nakedness, its bulk, its realism," and acknowledged it as the equivalent of "the most discussed picture of the year."[66] But Rivers's most confrontational painting would be his *Double Portrait of Berdie* of 1955 (cat. 71), which hit New York with what Allan Frumkin remembers as "stunning force."[67]

The painting was disturbing on several counts: it was a naturalistic figure painting executed by an avant-garde artist; it contained two distinct images of the same individual, which mitigated against a straightforward reading; and it delineated a woman whose age and weight were at a far remove from classical canons of female beauty. While de Kooning's *Marilyn Monroe* confronted viewers with the archetype of feminine

Larry Rivers
Augusta, 1954
oil on canvas
83 x 53 inches
Collection of the artist

Willem de Kooning
Marilyn Monroe, 1954
oil on canvas
50 x 30 inches
Collection of Neuberger Museum, State
University of New York at Purchase, Gift
of Roy R. Neuberger

pulchritude transformed by his spontaneous, gestural style, Rivers's *Berdie* assaulted his audience with an image of a compliant, perfectly ordinary older woman, a symbol of nothing save that which was universally regarded as an unworthy subject of esthetic attention. In his critique of the painting for *Arts Magazine*, Leo Steinberg panned it, focusing on the disjuncture of subject and style. He faulted the picture for coupling "genuine nastiness . . . with false charm,"[68] for combining the delineation of the sitter, "painted with so clinical an eye for obnoxious detail," with "the milder eye" of a decorative painter evident in the rugs, coverlets and background still life. He found it was the "lack of intrinsic esthetic unity . . . which makes the total absence of compassion in the rendering of Berdie so revolting."

Unlike Larry Rivers, Fairfield Porter and Alex Katz, who never worked abstractly, George McNeil came to the figure at the end of the fifties. Even at that late date, McNeil felt the onus against figuration within the New York avant-garde. Some of his friends regarded his new work as a betrayal:

> I remember I said something someone didn't like, not having to do with figuration, and he said, "Well, you're painting *figures* now." I was absolutely astonished.[69]

Twenty years previously he had flirted with social realism: "I wanted to paint cops standing on the necks of strikers, and I couldn't do it." But in the fifties, he began to feel that "art should have a deeper meaning than pure form and should go into some kind of a human direction." In 1958 McNeil joined a group organized by painter Mercedes Matter that gathered weekly to draw from the model. With hindsight, he is aware that this exposure "surely had a practical relation to my going into figuration."

Looking back, McNeil is now cognizant of an early ambivalence during the thirties, when he "alternated between carefully shaping almost pure abstractions and spontaneously painting semifigurative subject matter and abstractions."[70] His move into figuration was gradual, and he didn't stop making abstractions until 1962: "Every year the figure came out more and more. At that point [of painting *Luciana*, 1960 (cat. 45)] I wouldn't know [at the onset] if I were making an abstraction or a figurative painting, but that unconscious impulse got stronger and stronger."

Since his student days with Hofmann, McNeil set up still lifes as a starting point for all his paintings, a practice he continued until the late seventies. His method was to "seize" the figure from the still life. What he painted often depended on his unconscious intentions: "They say that the wish is the father to the thought. When I was thinking about abstraction, I would see abstractions; when I was thinking about figures, then I would see figures."

Robert Goodnough, who like George McNeil was a former Hofmann student, vacillated between abstraction and figuration in the late fifties. In a 1958 statement for *It is*, he wrote about his need for release from imposed conventions of the object:

> The composition, it seemed, should not be unalterably determined by what one was looking at and attempting to paint. . . . Gradually the subject, a group of figures or a street scene, was ignored or taken apart and the shapes rearranged to form a more stable design and the subject itself might disappear or emerge in a new way. Or a painting might be started without a particular subject in mind, and a relationship of shapes might suggest an idea. This idea could be abstract (or without recognizable objects) or it could develop into recognizable things. A great deal of freedom was then possible at the outset of the painting.[71]

In Goodnough's view, all of his paintings of that time, even those which may seem nonobjective, are figurative images.[72]

If the New York figurative expressionists of the fifties shaped their art in relation to abstract expressionism, then so too did their contemporaries Jasper Johns and Robert Rauschenberg. Attention to the work of these two seminal artists grew in the early sixties, when the prevailing taste shifted toward a cooler, less emotive style that addressed an allusive, pop culture content. Interest in figural expressionism waned as the new phenomenon of pop art began to capture the public imagination. Lester Johnson sensed this as early as 1959, when, as a panel participant with Allan Kaprow, Claes Oldenburg and Jim Dine on "New Uses of the Human Image in Painting" at New York's Judson Gallery, he felt himself treated as irrelevant by the audience. He recalls that at about that time, whenever he gave a public talk, he purposely used the word "passion" to set himself apart from the growing coolness of the art he saw around him.[73] Expressionism was no longer fashionable. An artist like Philip Pearlstein, who himself had early been an expressionist but not yet a figurative painter, now railed against the "New York artists who use the excuse of love for humanity to imbed ideograms of sad looking people in otherwise standard Action Painting."[74]

In 1957 New York's Jewish Museum put on a ground-breaking exhibition, *The New York School; Second Generation: Paintings by Twenty-three Artists*, which had included representational paintings by Grace Hartigan, Lester Johnson, Wolf Kahn, Jan Müller, Felix Pasilis and George Segal. In the four years between 1959 and 1962, the rest of the museum community caught up with the figural developments in New York School painting. In 1959, the Museum of Modern Art mounted *New Images of Man*, a thematic exhibition based on the subject of the human form. Of the twenty-three European, Bay Area, Chicago and New York painters and sculptors included in this unwieldy and idiosyncratic selection, only three were New York School figurative expressionists—Willem de Kooning, Jan Müller, and Jackson Pollock. *New Images* represented the museum's delayed acknowledgement that figurative art in the postwar period had not been obliterated by the overwhelming persuasiveness of American abstraction. Yet while many who felt they had been out in the cold for too long took heart, others expressed skepticism that the show was "the 'long awaited' answer to Abstract Expressionism."[75] Several observers concluded that the "effigies of the disquiet man,"[76] which curator Peter Selz had isolated, constituted too narrow a definition of contemporary figuration. As Sidney Tillim archly observed two years later, *New Images* "isolated the virus of despair as the reason why certain artists throughout the world, from Dubuffet to Diebenkorn, beat up on the image the way they do."[77]

Several related exhibitions followed in the wake of *New Images*. In 1960 the American Federation of the Arts organized a traveling exhibition called *The Figure in Contemporary American Painting*, comprised of many Bay Area and New York painters, including Lester Johnson, Jan Müller, Fairfield Porter, Larry Rivers and Bob Thompson. Houston's Contemporary Arts Museum assembled an all American group of nineteen painters for their 1961 *The Emerging Figure*, including Willem de Kooning, Lester Johnson, Alex Katz and Jan Müller. Curator

Donald Barthelme, in an introductory statement, spoke of "the sudden prominence" of the figure as an organizing principle "in the work of the children of the de Kooning generation."[78] The Guggenheim Museum's 1962 retrospective of Jan Müller, four years after his untimely death, further enhanced public awareness of the importance of the figure to the avant-garde.

The Museum of Modern Art sponsored a second exhibition focusing on figuration in 1962. *Recent Painting USA: The Figure* was a juried competition which drew nearly 2,000 entrants, from whom 74 were selected, including Robert Beauchamp, Elaine de Kooning, Lester Johnson and Larry Rivers. "The mere fact of the show," noted *Time* magazine, signaled the prominence of "a new kind of U.S. representationalism," whose excitement "traces back to abstraction."[79] While some in the artist community praised it for its democratic and national selection process,[80] others took offense that it wasn't a curated show, as it would have been had the organizing theme been abstraction.[81] Alex Katz, for example, refused to apply, despite the urging of Frank O'Hara, one of the jurors.[82]

Many in the New York art world felt that the Museum of Modern Art had again slighted the achievements of the New York School figurative expressionists and resolved to rectify matters with an all-New-York show entitled *The Figure*, which opened the same night as *Recent Painting U.S.A*. This salon-style show at the Kornblee Gallery was sponsored by twelve major galleries. Jack Kroll, in his introduction to the catalog, stressed the continuity of figuration and abstraction in modernism and, in an apparent reference to *New Images*, wrote: "Today the figure painters are just as polemical about the death of humanism as the abstract painters, perhaps more so, and they are just as circumpsect about resuscitating it." Among the twenty-two painters exhibiting were Robert Beauchamp, Elaine de Kooning, Robert Goodnough, Lester Johnson, Alex Katz, Fairfield Porter and Larry Rivers.

1962 was the last year for major exhibitions of figurative expressionsim. Subsequently, if museums thought about the figure in relation to the New York School, it was solely in terms of the prototypes and embodiment of pop art. Such was the influential power and international presence of the new

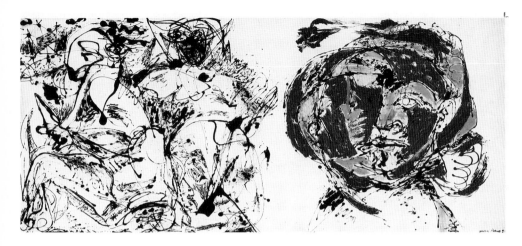

Jackson Pollock
Portrait and a Dream, 1953
enamel on canvas
58⅛ x 134⅜ inches
Collection Dallas Museum of Art, gift of
Mr. and Mrs. Algur H. Meadows and the
Meadows Foundation Incorporated

realism, as pop art was also called, that it came to be regarded by many as the legitimate successor to abstract expressionism. The apotheosis of this attitude was Henry Geldzahler's 1970 exhibition at the Metropolitan Museum, *New York Painting and Sculpture: 1940-1970*. Of the 408 works in this bellwether show, only one could properly be described as an example of fifties expressionist figuration, namely Jackson Pollock's majestic *Portrait and a Dream* of 1953, which was half abstract. Among the twelve paintings by de Kooning, three were figurative images from the forties; his germinal fifties Women were noticeably absent. In his catalog essay, Geldzahler diffidently anticipated his antagonists:

> There were critics in the fifties crying for a return to the figure, for a "new humanism." What they were hoping for was something comfortable and recognizable, a resuscitation of the art of the past veiled in the flaying brushstrokes of Abstract Expressionism. When they got their new figuration, it was not the tortured humanism of the postnuclear world for which they were longing but an art based on billboards, comic strips, and advertising.[83]

Geldzahler's curatorial selection of the New York School clearly reflected Clement Greenberg's early conviction that abstraction was the major mode of the period and that all other modes were necessarily minor.

This rigid characterization of the fifties seems less convincing at a distance of nearly four decades. The New York School painters who used the figure compositionally and thematically saw no essential difference in rank between abstraction and figuration. Some chose the figure from the start, others slowly gravitated toward it, and still others shifted back and forth between abstraction and representation out of internal necessity. As historians of the eighties in the process of figuring out the fifties, it is time to revise our comprehension of the period by looking more closely at what the artists themselves said and did. ■

The author gratefully expresses her appreciation to Sarah McFadden, Frank Goodyear, Harry Gaugh, and Susan Danly for their helpful comments on the first draft of this essay. Pennsylvania Academy librarian Marietta Bushnell merits special thanks for facilitating research by her numerous kindnesses.

Notes

1. Alex Katz, in conversation with the author and Paul Schimmel, February 3, 1988.

2. Throughout this essay the term "abstraction" will be used synonymously with "nonfigurative," "nonrepresentational" and "nonobjective," following the changed identity of the word in the fifties; see Lawrence Campbell, *Nell Blaine* (Richmond: Virginia Museum, 1973), p. 7.

3. John Ashbery, "Jane Freilicher," *Jane Freilicher* (New York: Taplinger Publishing Co., 1986), p. 21.

4. Lawrence Campbell, "Reviews and Previews, Grace Hartigan," *Art News* 54 (March 1955), pp. 51-52.

5. Elaine de Kooning, "Subject: What, How or Who?", *Art News* 54 (March 1955), p. 26.

6. Clement Greenberg, "Abstract, Representational, and So Forth," *Art and Culture* (Boston: Beacon Press, 1961), p. 133.

7. Grace Hartigan, in conversation with the author, January 26, 1988.

8. Fairfield Porter, "Conversation with Fairfield Porter," conducted by Paul Cummings, in *Fairfield Porter* (Boston: Museum of Fine Arts, 1982), p. 56.

9. The text of this "most celebrated anecdote in connection with Porter's career," was discussed by Hilton Kramer in "Fairfield Porter: An American Classic," *The New Criterion* (May 1983), p. 5. In response to Kramer's essay, Clement Greenberg wrote to the editor to deny that Porter introduced him to de Kooning and to declare that he would never speak to an artist in the manner recounted by Porter. In Greenberg's description, Fairfield Porter was "an inveterate prevaricator," *The New Criterion* (September 1983), p. 88. In letters to the editor published two months later, Alex Katz expressed shock at Greenberg's contradictions of Porter, and Rackstraw Downes defended the veracity of Porter's account, indicating that de Kooning too recalled the incident. For Downes, Porter's telling of his reaction to the interchange in de Kooning's studio was "a serious joke," *The New Criterion* (November 1983), pp. 90-91.

10. Thomas B. Hess, *De Kooning: Recent Paintings* (New York: Walker and Company, 1967), p. 40.

11. Robert Goodnough, in conversation with the author and Paul Schimmel, February 2, 1988.

12. "Editorial," *Reality, A Journal of Artists' Opinions* (Spring 1954), p. 2.

13. Ibid.

14. Ibid., p. 8.

15. Ibid., pp. 10 and 7.

16. Philip Pavia, "An Open Letter to Leslie Katz, Publisher of *Arts Magazine*, New York City," *It is* (Autumn 1959), p. 79.

17. The cooperative Hansa Gallery, named in honor of Hans Hofmann, was founded in 1952 by Miles Forst, Wolf Kahn, Jan Müller, and Felix Pasilis. See Irving Sandler, *The New York School* (New York: Harper and Row, 1978), p. 36.

18. Martica Sawin, "Jan Müller: 1922-1958," *Arts Magazine* 33 (February 1959), p. 39.

19. Literary historian Marjorie Perloff has made a convincing argument that O'Hara's poems on the work of Hartigan and Rivers reveal "that he was really more at home with painting that retains at least some figuration than with pure abstraction." Marjorie Perloff, *Frank O'Hara: Poet Among Painters* (New York: George Braziller, 1977), p. 85.

20. Frank O'Hara, "Nature and New Painting," *Folder*, no. 3 (1954-55), n.p., facsimile reprinted in *Art with the Touch of a Poet* (Benton Gallery, University of Connecticut, 1983). Subsequent quotations of O'Hara in this and the following paragraph are from this source.

21. Thomas B. Hess, "The Many Deaths of American Art," *Art News* 59 (October 1960), p. 25.

22. Thomas B. Hess, "U.S. Painting, Some Recent Directions," *Art News Annual* (1956), p. 76.

23. Dody Müller, in conversation with the author, January 31, 1988.

24. Grace Hartigan, in conversation with the author, January 26, 1988.

25. For her February 1950 *Art News* article "Hans Hofmann Paints a Picture," she recalls that she visited with Hofmann on at least ten occasions to gather material; Elaine de Kooning, in conversation with the author and Paul Schimmel, February 5, 1988.

26. For a complete discussion of Hofmann's method, see Cynthia Good-

man, *The Hans Hofmann School and Hofmann's Transmission of European Modernist Aesthetics*, unpublished Ph.D. dissertation, The University of Pennsylvania, 1982.

27. Wolf Kahn, in "Hans Hofmann Student Dossier," unpublished typescript compiled by William Seitz (New York: Museum of Modern Art Library, 1963), n.p.

28. Hess, "U.S. Painting, Some Recent Directions," *Art News Annual*, p. 95.

29. Hans Hofmann quoted in Elaine de Kooning, "Hans Hofmann Paints a Picture," *Art News* 48 (February 1950), pp. 38-41.

30. Red Grooms, in conversation with the author, December 1984.

31. John Bernard Myers, *Tracking the Marvelous* (New York: Random House, 1983), p. 121.

32. Larry Rivers, "A Discussion of the Work of Larry Rivers," *Art News* (March 1961), p. 121.

33. Dody Müller, in conversation with the author, January 31, 1988.

34. Jan Müller quoted in "Airless Despair," *Time* (February 2, 1962), p. 44.

35. Robert Beauchamp, quoted in "The Reappearing Figure," *Time* (May 25, 1962), p. 62.

36. Philip Pearlstein, Lois Dodd, Sally Hazelet, "All Beauchamp!!" *Scrap* (December 9, 1960), p. 3.

37. Lester Johnson, in conversation with the author and Paul Schimmel, February 3, 1988.

38. Meyer Levin, "Exhibit By Young Artists," unidentified clipping in the collection of Lester Johnson, and Meyer Levin and Eli Levin, "Johnson Is Hailed by 'Avant Garde,'" *The Philadelphia Inquirer*, April 12, 1959.

39. Sidney Geist, *Artforum* 26 (February 1988), p. 84.

40. Johnson was the only artist to have shown there during every season of its operation, and was honored with a special three-week retrospective in 1957; see *The Sun Gallery*, exhibition catalog, Provincetown Art Association and Museum, 1981, p. 17.

41. Earlier that winter, Johnson, Grooms, Andersen and Falcone had teamed up to assemble a portfolio of text and images entitled *City*, which had been printed and assembled by Yvonne and contained poems by Val, reproductions of charcoal studies by Lester, and ink drawings by Red; reproduced in *Red Grooms: A Retrospective, 1956-1984* (Philadelphia: Pennsylvania Academy of the Fine Arts, 1985), p. 33.

42. George Segal, quoted in Graham W.J. Beal, "Realism at a Distance," *George Segal: Sculptures* (Minneapolis: Walker Art Center, 1978), p. 62.

43. Lester Johnson, in conversation with the author, February 9, 1988, and Alfred Leslie, in conversation with the author, February 9, 1988.

44. Robert Beauchamp, in conversation with the author and Paul Schimmel, January 30, 1988.

45. This understanding of Pollock's working method is derived from obser-

vations by Lee Krasner; see Elizabeth Frank, *Jackson Pollock* (New York: Abbeville Press, 1983), p. 90.

46. Jackson Pollock, quoted in Elizabeth Frank, *Jackson Pollock*, p. 95.

47. Dody Müller, in conversation with the author, January 31, 1988.

48. Robert Goodnough, quoted in Martin Bush, *Goodnough* (New York: Abbeville, 1982), p. 69.

49. Dody Müller, in conversation with the author, January 31, 1988.

50. Hess, "U.S. Painting: Some Recent Directions," *Art News Annual*, p. 194.

51. Valerie Petersen, "U.S. Figure Painting: Continuity and Cliche," *Art News* 61 (Summer 1962), p. 52.

52. Philip Pearlstein, "Figure Paintings Today Are Not Made in Heaven," *Art News* 61 (Summer 1962), p. 52.

53. Leo Steinberg, "De Kooning's *Woman*," *Other Criteria* (London: Oxford University Press, 1972), p. 260.

54. Thomas B. Hess, "Mixed Pickings from the Fat Years," *Art News* 54 (Summer 1955), p. 78.

55. Manny Farber, "New Images of (ugh) Man," *Art News* 58 (October 1959), p. 39.

56. Fairfield Porter, "Conversation with Fairfield Porter," in *Fairfield Porter* (exhibition catalog), p. 53.

57. Mrs. Fairfield Porter, in conversation with the author and Paul Schimmel, February 5, 1988.

58. Elaine de Kooning, in conversation

with the author and Paul Schimmel, February 5, 1988.

59. Elaine de Kooning, "Statement," *It is* (Autumn 1959), pp. 29-30.

60. Alex Katz, quoted in Edwin Denby, "Katz: Collage, Cutout, Cutup," [1965], in Irving Sandler and Bill Berkson, eds., *Alex Katz* (New York: Praeger, 1971), p. 35.

61. Selden Rodman, *Conversations with Artists* (New York: The Devin-Adair Co., 1957), p. 115.

62. Larry Rivers, quoted in *Conversations with Artists*, p. 117.

63. Seymour Remenick, quoted in "A Master Teacher [Hans Hofmann]," *Life* (April 8, 1957), p. 70.

64. Larry Rivers, in conversation with the author and Paul Schimmel, February 4, 1988.

65. Larry Rivers, "A Discussion of the Work of Larry Rivers," *Art News*, p. 54.

66. Lawrence Campbell, "New Figures at Uptown Whitney," *Art News* 53 (February 1955), pp. 34-35.

67. Allan Frumkin, "The Figurative Tradition," *Arts Magazine* 55 (September 1980), p. 9.

68. Leo Steinberg, "Month in Review," *Arts Magazine* 30 (January 1956), p. 48. Subsequent unidentified quotations in the paragraph are from this source.

69. George McNeil, in conversation with the author and Paul Schimmel, February 2, 1988. Unidentified quotations in the next two paragraphs are from this source.

70. George NcNeil, "One Painter's Expressionism," *George McNeil: Expressionism, 1954-1984* (New York: Artists' Choice Museum, 1984), p. 8.

71. Robert Goodnough, "Statement," *It is* (Spring 1958), p. 46.

72. Robert Goodnough, in conversation with the author and Paul Schimmel, February 2, 1988.

73. Lester Johnson, in conversation with the author and Paul Schimmel, February 3, 1988.

74. Philip Pearlstein, "Figure Paintings Today Are Not Made in Heaven," *Art News*, p. 51.

75. Manny Farber, "New Images of (ugh) Man," *Art News*, p. 58.

76. Peter Selz, "Introduction," *New Images of Man* (New York: Museum of Modern Art, 1961), p. 12.

77. Sidney Tillim, "The Present Outlook on Figurative Painting," *Arts Yearbook* 5 (1961), p. 38.

78. D[onald] B[arthelme], [Introduction], *The Emerging Figure* (Houston: Contemporary Arts Museum, 1961), n.p.

79. "The Reappearing Figure," *Time* (May 25, 1962), p. 62.

80. This was particularly true for artists who lived outside of New York, such as Philadelphian Sidney Goodman, who was 26 at the time of his inclusion in this exhibition; Sidney Goodman, conversation with the author, February 20, 1988.

81. Speaking ostensibly for New York-based painters, Valerie Petersen observed that "artists who should have been included were not invited and felt it demeaning to file a formal request for consideration, did not want to have their work judged by a photograph, were unaware of the 'contest,' were too lazy to fill out the application or were opposed in principle to this outdated means of organizing an exhibition," "U.S. Figure Painting: Continuity and Cliche," *Art News* 61 (Summer 1962), p. 51.

82. Alex Katz, in conversation with the author and Paul Schimmel, February 3, 1988.

83. Henry Geldzahler, "New York School Painting and Sculpture: 1940-1970," *New York School Painting and Sculpture: 1940-1970* (New York: The Metropolitan Museum of Art, 1970), pp. 35-36.

The Women

Paul Schimmel

Willem de Kooning's Woman paintings of 1949-54 were the most invigorating contribution to the figurative wave of the 1950s, and their significance is even more evident today. De Kooning's move back to the figure at the beginning of that decade was a brilliant counterpoint to his breakthrough black and white abstractions of the late forties and opened an avenue of investigation that used figurative armature to ground a dialog between representation and abstract form. Although his renewed interest in the figure was seen in some quarters as a retreat to preabstract figuration and a threat to New York's hard-won status as the premier city of international art, many of the artists of the fifties felt liberated by it from the canon of "pure" abstraction.[1] De Kooning's switch undermined the critical belief that art history was on an inevitable march toward reductionist tendencies. But de Kooning was not a politician taking the pulse of the ever-changing vagaries of the art world; for him the reintroduction of figurative elements provided, first, structure and, second, subject to the gestural and formal strides he had achieved in such paintings as *Dark Pond* (1948) and *Attic* (1949).

To those who saw the Women at Sidney Janis Gallery in 1953 or read Thomas Hess's coinciding article "De Kooning Paints a Picture" in *Art News*, it was a shocker.[2] To the viewer with a short memory, de Kooning's break with the accomplishments of abstraction seemed a calculated move to unsettle the tradition of the new. For New York even mildly to acknowledge the European figurative tradition (e.g., Chaim Soutine) was to tromp on the seedling of America's artistic dominance, to give away the country after having won the war, a reversal in the avant-garde. But that was grist for the critic's mill. The debate between Rosenberg and Greenberg over critical approaches was just that, a critical debate; it wasn't about painting. Certainly artists could use this controversy to position themselves in the crossfire, bringing attention to themselves and their work (e.g., Larry Rivers), but that was outside the studio. For de Kooning it was the studio that counted. Time would take care of the critics.

In de Kooning's work the dialog was not about art history, abstraction, or the figure for that matter, but about painting. It was about working in an abstract mode until the cubist armature had been lost in gesture, and out of the gesture (the act of painting) pulling the image back through the figurative tradition—a tradition in de Kooning's work which had been

there from the start. In the thirties, after a period of work in the abstract manner of Picasso as seen through Gorky and Graham, he returned to the figure and the line of Ingres that he admired so much, as evidenced in his *Self-Portrait with Imaginary Brother* (c. 1938). During the forties, when other first-generation abstract artists were working in an abstract-surrealist mode using organic and primordial imagery, de Kooning was painting curvilinear, biomorphic, semiabstract figurative work (e.g., *The Queen of Hearts*, c. 1943, and *Pink Angels*, c. 1945). His return to the figure was a means of reintroducing three-dimensional space in order to battle against it.

Why the subject of the woman? The familiar and sensual form of woman became the structure with which he could expand his extraordinary visual and technical skills. One should take at face value de Kooning's belief that the curvilinear form of a woman's buttocks, waist, hips and breasts provided a natural starting point from which the gestural application of paint could bring together subject, form and stylistic technique. One can't just slop paint on canvas in a bravura of technical facility; a painter needs some subject, a content to temper his visceral experience.

Over the years there has been much speculation as to who the women are that de Kooning depicts. There is certainly no definitive answer. One can speculate that the eyes are the large Armenian eyes of Gorky's women of the thirties, that the mouth is Marilyn Monroe's or the toothy smile of some other pin-up girl, that the body is the archetype of the American sex goddess as conquerer of the male ego—all these things could be true; or one can see the features as choices the artist made during the expressionist, gestural act of painting. In the infamous Rudy Burckhardt series of photographs of six stages of *Woman I* (1950-52) one realizes that the artist needed to flatten the picture plane and to eliminate background detail in order to find an expression in the woman's face as vigorous and fierce as the brushstrokes that made it.

The Woman series comprises at least three phases. The first phase, 1949-51, is characterized by multiple investigations occurring simultaneously, including aspects of the biomorphic elements of *Pink Angels*, the cubist chiseled faceting of the figure on the picture plane, and the use of collage-like printed

elements. The raging, anguished figures appear to have antecedents in Picasso's *Guernica*. At the same time de Kooning began painting the Women, he was also painting his most accomplished abstractions, the black and white canvases whose kidney-shaped elements interlock in an overall pattern of line and gesture. The next important direction in his work, which culminated in the Museum of Modern Art's masterpiece *Woman I* (1950-52), is already evident in the more Soutine-inspired *Woman* (1949-50) (cat. 12). In this work, the startled figure with arms raised is immersed in a predominantly black and white background of gesture; like Soutine's hanging carcasses (c. 1924-26), de Kooning's figure is composed of disjunctive body parts that weave in front of and behind the picture plane.

In *Untitled Study, Woman (3 Women)* (n.d.) (cat. 9), the three archaic figures are executed in black and white, giving the work the quality of a cubist/futurist sculpture in white marble. The ground of color is reminiscent of de Kooning's nonobjective, biomorphic abstractions of the thirties. De Kooning's usual balance in single and double figure compositions is disturbed in this unique three-figure work, and the central figure has its head twisted in anguish and its back to the viewer.

In *Two Women on a Wharf* (1949) (cat. 10), de Kooning employs a collage-like technique, repeating and overlaying figurative elements. The figure on the right has three pairs of breasts repeated vertically on the canvas. In this work, two years in advance of the 1950-52 *Woman I* painting, de Kooning already incorporates many of the key elements and painterly techniques that he uses consistently throughout the Woman series. Beginning with a fractured cubist composition, he disrupts the linear aspect of the figure with broad strokes of pure color. Working with high-keyed greens and pinks, he seems to have collaged gestures and slashes of paint onto the surface. Although the figures are indicative of the later Woman paintings, the faces are less distinctly in de Kooning's signature; the organic, biomorphic features of the face on the left, for example, are reminiscent of Picasso's surrealist *Bathers* (c. 1930-32). While incorporating aspects of the black and white abstractions, *Woman* (1949-50) (cat. 12) leads the way both in scale and frontality to the mature Woman works. A large-scale, jagged, aggressive composition with stronger linear than coloristic elements, this Woman stands halfway between the early

Willem de Kooning
Attic, 1949
oil on canvas
61⅛ x 80¼ inches
Jointly owned by The Metropolitan
Museum of Art and Muriel Kallis Newman,
in honor of her son Glenn David Steinberg;
The Muriel Kallis Steinberg Newman
Collection, 1982

and middle periods. The figure and ground are inseparable in parts of the composition, and the biomorphic sensuality so prevalent in the Women of the middle phase is less evident here than the gritty process of alternately revealing and obliterating the central figure.

The smaller oil on paper and board works of the earliest phase of the Woman series reveal more about de Kooning's working methods than the finished "masterpieces" of the same years. In each small oil on paper de Kooning explores one aspect of his concerns rather than synthesizes a multitude of investigations in large canvases composed over an extended period of time. In *Warehouse Mannequins* (1949) (cat. 11), a simple biomorphic composition, the figures separate into body parts, with the unconnected head, buttocks and breasts arranged horizontally across the picture plane. Although the body shapes refer to the more sensuous biomorphic figures of the thirties, the face with V-shaped eyes and a sinister, toothy grin is typical of the mature Woman paintings.

The year 1952, the beginning of the middle phase of the Woman series, was an extraordinarily successful year for de Kooning. *Two Women with Still Life* (1952) (cat. 16) is one of the most beautiful, rich, sensual pastels in de Kooning's oeuvre. Two full-length standing figures emerge from a richly hued ground that suggests the color scheme of nature—the blue of sky, the green of foliage, the brown of earth. While distinctly de Kooning, this masterpiece has as its compositional equivalent Gorky's great *Study for "The Liver is the Cock's Comb"* (1943), based on the Virginia landscape. An extraordinary range of colors is lovingly interwoven in *Two Women with Still Life*, which incorporates elements of landscape and still life (as seen in the elements in the lower portion of the composition) with two large, cycladic, frontal figures of women. The woman on the right is blatantly female with large hips and breasts and a tightly drawn waist. The lips are full, red and sensual. The figure on the left, although clearly also female, hints at androgyny with its broad chest and thick waist. The buttocks, so clear on the right figure, are less pronounced on the left figure, and the voluptuousness of the right form contrasts with the muscularity of that on the left.

Two Women (1952) (cat. 17), another mature work from the middle phase, excels in its linear strength and the architectural framing around the figure. Similar in composition to *Two Women with Still Life*, this pencil and crayon drawing is a harder, more angular work in its unusually forceful use of diagonal lines in the background, the figure, and even the paper; the drawing is cut at an angle across the bottom, cropping the feet and accentuating the angularity of the composition.

While the first phase of the Woman series is characterized by a multiplicity of stylistic elements drawn from de Kooning's enormous resources and the second phase brackets the most original, accomplished and linear examples of the Women, the third phase, 1953-55, evidences a more frequent use of pure color that is less descriptive of subject. Increasingly, de Kooning applies paint directly on paper and canvas without using pencil or charcoal to define the figure. The works begin to take on the quality of woman-as-landscape rather than woman-in-landscape. These latter Women anticipate de Kooning's move back to abstraction, not in blacks and whites as in the late forties, but in the riotous color that foreshadows his "urban landscape" paintings of the mid-fifties. Eliminating descriptive detail, he concentrates on the breasts exclusively in *Arrangement in Pink and Green* (1955) (cat. 23). In *Woman* (1955) (cat. 24) only the eyes and breasts are distinctly legible, with an ovoid shape in the appropriate location representing at the mouth. The turquoise, shocking pinks, and garish reds are increasingly independent of the subjects and less suggestive of human coloration. After 1955 de Kooning concentrated primarily on landscapes of both New York and his home in eastern Long Island.

De Kooning's natural evolution from black and white abstractions through the figure to his coloristically charged landscapes of the latter half of the fifties was, for many of the artists in this exhibition, a revelation of the working process of an artist they held in the highest esteem.

It wasn't how the Women paintings were executed that so disturbed the critics; it was that they had a subject. For many, de Kooning's exclusive focus on women as subjects was a matter for great speculation. Who were these women, and what did they mean? Why did they look so fierce and simultaneously sensual? Were they a reflection of personal turmoil in the artist's life? Were they a symbol of the American woman, the pin-up girl? There will never be a concrete answer to these questions because the Women are first and foremost part of a formal painterly evolution in de Kooning's work. The "subject of the artist" was paint, not, as has been speculated, images of Elaine with whom he was married through 1956, nor his mother, nor the archetypal, postwar, liberated American woman. Phases in Picasso's career can be defined by the lovers and wives he had. With de Kooning, that specificity just doesn't exist.

Notes

1. Grace Hartigan in conversation with the author, January 26, 1988, and Larry Rivers in conversation with the author and Judith Stein, February 4, 1988.

2. The exhibition *Paintings on the Theme of Woman* was held at Sidney Janis Gallery, New York, March 16-April 11, 1953. Thomas B. Hess, "De Kooning Paints a Picture," *Art News* 52 (March 1953), pp. 30-33, 64-67.

Plates/Entries

Robert Beauchamp

The world Robert Beauchamp inhabits, the "floating world" he creates in his paintings, can be a frightening place. Not in a sci-fi sense and not in the distancing semi-safety of hobgoblins and monsters, but rather in a personal, interiorized, real way where we recognize the distortive power of our emotions. Ordinary, familiar things may suddenly seem menacing—a group of women dappled by black firelight may turn into witches, a common zoo animal or domestic pet may become subtly demonic—because we confront them in an abruptly different way. Then too, anomalous terrors do lurk beneath the surface of daily life. One of the artist's strongest memories from his Denver childhood concerns a woman who killed her husband by mixing ground glass in the sugar.

But Beauchamp is not a depictor; his unsettling images come to the surface unbidden, found largely by chance in the act of painting. Trained by Boardman Robinson to search for forms in the process of drawing and inspired by Hans Hofmann and other abstract expressionists to let the paint itself dictate many of his moves, he works as automatically as possible, giving accident more control than deliberation. For example, he didn't set out to paint a literal *Initiation* in the 1960 painting of that name. He was working light areas against dark, reds off greens, aligning tubular forms that happened to be leglike and paralleling amorphous curving shapes when they showed up in close proximity, as they do in the lower left corner. One pictorial element demanded the next in a generally figurative context.

The overall color-patch look of Beauchamp's late fifties figurative works was shared by the abstractionist graduates of the Hofmann school, all equally involved with Hofmann's push/pull, give-and-take method of building a painting. *Witches* and *Tournament of Witches*, both of 1959, give clear evidence of Beauchamp's "abstract" distribution of color areas all over the surface. The background of *Witches* is reduced to a few brilliant Gauguinesque primaries while smaller units dapple the simian creatures in the foreground. A swath of bright blue edging the left-hand figure's arm is echoed in the arm of the central figure and reiterated full blast in the animal-like figure on the right. Reds located spatially and laterally in the center of the painting are held to the picture plane by reds of like temperature placed to either side, in front and behind them.

Tournament of Witches, in fact, barely edges out of abstraction. In it, the spots of color coalesce into birds but might just as readily have become female figures—as some did—or animals. The artist's process of "seeing" an automatically arrived-at form as an arm, a belly, a face or a beak and then picking it out for emphasis is as completely arbitrary as that of a child finding monsters in the ceiling cracks or a dreamer seeing faces and animals in the clouds. Of course, as happens with Rorschach imagery, the choices the artist makes, as well as the interpretations the viewer puts on them, are fair game for analysis. What Beauchamp terms his "floating world" is a highly charged place of constant flux and rich emotional potential. The only fixed and certain aspect of his hybrid style is the excitement it generates. ■

April Kingsley

1   *Tournament of the Witches*,
1959
oil on canvas
60 x 69 inches
Collection The Chrysler
Museum, Norfolk, Virginia

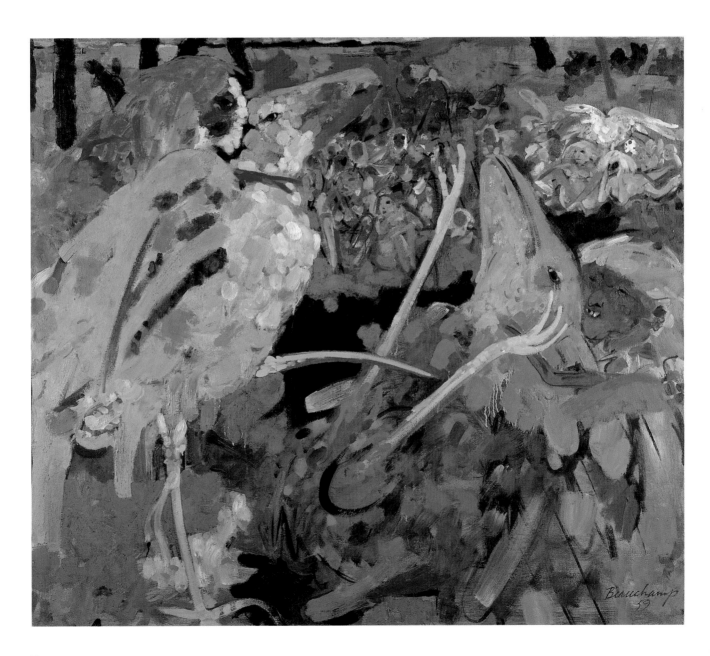

2 *Witches*, 1959
oil on canvas
36½ x 46½ inches
Collection Judith and Mitchell
Kramer

4 *Untitled*, 1963
oil on canvas
65¾ x 68 inches
Courtesy of the artist

3 *Untitled*, 1960
oil on canvas
71 ½ x 90 inches
Archer M. Huntington Art
Gallery, Univerisity of Texas at
Austin; Lent by James and
Mari Michener

Elaine de Kooning

Even during the 1950s Elaine de Kooning, in her thirties, was close to the heart of the New York art world. She had been painting seriously since her teens. She had studied mainly, and most rewardingly, with Willem de Kooning, and since 1943 she had been married to him. She was also writing frequent reviews and monographs for *Art News*. And finally, she was making figurative paintings at a time when doing so was considered unfashionable, if not retrogressive.

Elaine de Kooning's painting came first, but in the fifties her writing reached a larger audience, as did the fact of her marriage to a better known artist, sixteen years her senior. In those years, her being a woman, a writer and part of the rather disparagingly labeled "second generation" distracted many viewers from the work itself. Three decades later, however, we remember that Louise Bourgeois, Louise Nevelson, Lee Krasner, Joan Mitchell, Grace Hartigan, and Helen Frankenthaler, among many other vanguard artists, were women too; that Krasner and (somewhat later) Frankenthaler also married famous artists; that half of these women were "second genera-tion"; that other artists, including Robert Motherwell, Ad Reinhardt and Fairfield Porter, regularly wrote on art; and that, among the male leaders of the abstract expressionists, the works of both Willem de Kooning in his series of women and Jackson Pollock in many of his black-and-white images of the early fifties were figurative.

Thus placed, with admittedly broad strokes, it's time, high time, to look at Elaine de Kooning's work of the mid-fifties. Her portraits are typical not only of this period but of what has followed to the present. They are concerned with the essential, often generalized stance and gesture of men and animals, frequently in action, sometimes in equally "active," though thoughtful repose.

The figures in *High Man* (1954), inspired as much by El Greco's elongated figures as by newspaper photographs of basketball players, are all action and energy. The central figure is suspended in a jump shot, flanked on one side by two opposing players (one half-hidden) and on the other by a teammate. The movement of these athletes is accentuated by drips, splatters and free brushstrokes. The physicality of the paint—the pink flesh tones, the contrasting uniforms, the dark ball, the exploding light background—echoes the subject matter.

There is a remarkable continuity between the intelligent, decisive, split-second activity of athletes and that of the artists and writers with whom Elaine de Kooning has been close. In various paintings of her husband—like most of her portraits, preceded by pencil drawings—she exhibits far more interest in posture and gestural configuration than in detailed likeness. The virtually faceless figure in *Bill at St. Mark's* (c. 1956) is seated, yet one has a sense of contained energy, of a man in deep dark murky thought, about to leap from his seat, and of hands ready to attack a canvas. In several portraits of her husband, his hands are placed even more pugnaciously on his hips, and the palette is equally dark, often predominantly gray-green.

The particularized gesture is equally apparent in other portraits of the fifties. The writer and editor Thomas B. Hess appears both elegantly poised and somewhat tortured as he sits with one leg crossed over his knee and one hand crossed over the other, the tension of his limbs emphasized by a criss-cross pattern of brushstrokes. In contrast, the figure in *Kaldis in a Yellow Chair* (1954) is all comfortable weight, all head and torso, surrounded by a bulbous armchair, the sitter seems incapable of supporting himself on the foreshortened legs and diminutive feet tucked beneath him. And in her contrasting portrait of Fairfield Porter—this one done from life, with no preliminary drawings—the artist-writer is perched on a stool whose spindly

5   *High Man*, 1954
oil on canvas
79 x 53 inches
Courtesy of the artist

legs align with his dangling hands and separate his long and narrow, widespread legs.

If all of these images express degrees of tension and relaxation and of weight and lightness, none is more relaxed and weightless, paradoxically, than Elaine de Kooning's 1956 portrait of the critic Harold Rosenberg. In it Rosenberg's body seems to flow from his head as his arms flow along the arms of the chair in which he sits, holding a can of beer in one hand and dangling and flicking a cigarette in the other. The figure seems to float in an airy background of light reds and greens — colors free of contours — its body free of a head and more realistically treated than the figures in most of the other portraits. This freedom anticipates in many ways the quality of her more recent work — the earliest images of a bull in 1957 and again, more frequently, in works completed since her first visit to the Lascaux caves in 1983. Yes, the paradoxes continue: an even greater airiness and lightness, inspired by caves, and a weightlessness of spirit in mammoth bulls as in athletes and artists! ■

B.H. Friedman

7   *Harold Rosenberg #III*, 1956
oil on canvas
80 x 59 inches
Courtesy of the artist

6 *Kaldis in Yellow Chair*, 1954
oil on canvas
63 ¾ x 49 ¾ inches
Courtesy of the artist

8 *Bill at St. Marks*, c. 1956
oil on canvas
72 x 43½ inches
Courtesy of the artist

Willem de Kooning

In his "Woman" series (1950-53), Willem de Kooning flooded the plane of the canvas with a torrential liquid fury that literally and figuratively gave body to the acts of painting. Simultaneously figuring and disfiguring, creating and destroying, rejoicing in and recoiling from sensuousness, de Kooning forged a profound unity of the ecstatic erotics of art and flesh. The shock that greeted these paintings upon their exhibition in 1953 was largely attributed to de Kooning's apparent renunciation of the abstraction that had earlier gained him acclaim, together with such peers as Pollock, Rothko, and Still; but their ferocious humor and brazen vulgarity surely compounded their offensiveness; they look as though the Venus of Willendorf is going through the convulsions of being cloned with a 1950s streetwalker trying to look like Marilyn Monroe. The turbulent viscosity makes visually concrete the subject and the object of painting's struggle for identity. Paint and figure are inextricably bound in shifting layers of smear and leer, resolution and dissolution, joy and fear. Seldom has the cathartic and victimless violence of creation been so compellingly excavated. As the full title for their exhibition suggests, these are not representations of women but quite literally "Paintings on the Theme of the Woman."

It is one of the many ironies of modernism that it frequently performed its radical operations on one of Western painting's most loaded and traditional subjects—the female figure, starting with the (af)frontality of Manet's *Olympia*, proceeding to Cézanne's various *Bathers* and Picasso's *Les Demoiselles d'Avignon*, and then to Duchamp's *Nude Descending a Staircase*. The figure, especially the female nude, was virtually shunned by America's first generation of modernists and played only a minor role in the later development of the abstract expressionists, who generally moved into abstraction through a landscape orientation. The militant abstractionism engendered by the heroic, noncompositional painterliness of Newman's, Pollock's, and Still's paintings, as well as de Kooning's own black and white works shown in 1948, seemed to brook no reference to anything outside the world of the painting itself. So total did the victory of the new abstraction seem, in the late forties and early fifties, that de Kooning's "Woman" paintings would only be regarded as a grievous lapse. His bitch/goddesses of paint had seduced him into taking an absence without leave.

De Kooning had, of course, never renounced the figure, just as he had never renounced his European roots. His painterliness did not so much spurn personal touch as completely reinvigorate it. Not only cubist underpinnings but reverberations of Rembrandt, Rubens and Van Gogh remained in much of de Kooning's work. If his exuberant physicality was more secular and less radical than that of Pollock and Still, it had the advantage of giving him more options to explore—options that, to this day, have not been exhausted. Picasso was as crucial to Pollock as to de Kooning, but de Kooning was less anxious to shut Picasso out. His "Woman" paintings hold up a mirror of painterliness to *Les Demoiselles d'Avignon* and dissolve its glacial angles and sculptural chiaroscuro in a near-lascivious liquidity.

Rudolph Burckhardt's photographs of the early stages of *Woman I* document the figure's gradual and frantic emergence from a cocoon of shifting angular and organic slabs related to de Kooning's early abstract masterpiece *Excavation* (1950) and to analytical cubism's shallow space structured with vacillating planes. The heated urgency to become is still fully evident in the final and visible layers of the "finished" painting, but is now enlivened by the fully ripened, lavish viscosity that would mark de Kooning's paintings for some time to come. The startling variety of the frenetic strokes and structure and the gritty density of the "Woman" paintings shifted back into a more abstract mode in the mid-fifties in such paintings as *Gotham News* and *Easter Monday* (both 1955-56). The breathlessly risky, kaleidoscopic instability that characterizes so many of de Kooning's paintings need only be twisted slightly to slip from figure to abstraction to near-landscape, to one or another hybrid of all three. In the mid-sixties, the figure would rise to the surface again, but now with a less violent and speedier zestfulness.

9 *Untitled Study, Woman (3 Women)*, n.d.
oil on paper
20⅜ x 26⅜ inches
Vassar College Art Gallery, Poughkeepsie, N.Y., Gift of Mrs. Richard Deutsch (Katherine W. Sandford '40), 53.2.5

The art world largely resisted De Kooning's refusal to accept distinctions between abstraction and figuration, present from the outset of his maturity, until the mid-seventies, but it now all but takes it for granted. In the late thirties and very early forties, his figurative and abstract works were more distinctly separate. They moved back and forth from exquisitely drawn and defined isolated figures hovering in a moody monochrome of alienation to a more impastoed, flat, Miro-and-Picasso-inspired biomorphic abstraction, often employing the lurid oranges, yellows and pinks that still punctuate de Kooning's palette. By the mid-forties, both the figurative and the abstract paintings began to loosen their clear contours, and the borders between the two modes began to blur as both surrendered their bodies to the making visible of the vagaries of the painting's procedures (surrealist automatism unnerved and decomposed the lyric rigors of Ingres). The disheveled representationalism of the seated female figure in *Pink Lady* (c. 1944) is only slightly more contained than the floating limbs and torso-like shapes in the more abstract *Pink Angels* (c. 1945). As line gained greater velocity and physical force, both the human and the abstract forms dissolved into pure figures of paint. Save for an agitated stroke or two, it is hard to say what makes *Two Women on a Wharf* (1949) more figurative than the abstract *Asheville* (1949). In *Woman* (1949-50), the full liberation of oil paint's fluid physicality and the deep urge to retrieve an order out of chaos turn the canvas into the pulsating chant of ecstasy and despair that would gain its full force and breadth in the succeeding "Woman" series (1950-53).

10 *Two Women on a Wharf*,
1949
oil, enamel, paper and collage
on paper
24½ x 24½ inches
Collection Art Gallery of
Ontario, Toronto, Canada;
Purchase, Membership Endowment Fund, 1977

Although Dutch born, de Kooning shares with many American painters, especially with his peers Pollock and Kline, a strong dependence on line and the will to propel drawing into painting. His extraordinary draughtsmanship is largely responsible for holding his paintings in tension and rescuing them from the messy void he risks and challenges. His many drawings of women done in the early and mid-fifties rank as some of the finest in a body of graphic work that stands among the most compelling of this (or any) century. In these drawings, the highly refined, sinuous tautness of his earlier Ingresque drawings is combined with and subverted by driving aleatory gestures that are seemingly unmediated enactments of the primal need to make a mark and claim space and form. Like the paintings, they are visceral records of and metaphors for the dilemmas of being and becoming. ∎

Klaus Kertess

12 *Woman*, 1949-50
oil on canvas
64 x 46 inches
Permanent Collection of the
Weatherspoon Art Gallery, The
University of North Carolina at
Greensboro, Lena Kernodle
McDuffie Memorial Gift

13 *Reclining Woman*, 1951
pencil on paper
8 ⅞ x 11 ¾ inches
Private Collection

11 *Warehouse Mannequins*,
1949
oil on board
24 x 34½ inches
Collection Mr. and Mrs.
Bagley Wright

15 *Woman*, c. 1951-52
graphite on paper, two-sided
drawing
12½ x 9½ inches
Private Collection

14 *Woman*, 1951
pastel and pencil on paper
11⅞ x 9½ inches
Collection Allan Stone Gallery

19 *Woman*, c. 1952-53
pastel and pencil on paper
16¼ x 14 inches
Collection Eve Propp

16 *Two Women with Still Life*, 1952
pastel on paper
22¼ x 24 inches
Collection Marcia S. Weisman

18   *Woman*, 1952-53
charcoal, crayon and collage
on paper
26 x 19 inches
Collection Dr. and Mrs. Martin
L. Gecht

17 *Two Women*, 1952
pencil on paper
12¾ x 12¾ inches
Collection Richard and Mary
L. Gray

21 *Woman I*, 1954
oil on canvas
25¾ x 19½ inches
Sheldon Memorial Art Gallery,
University of Nebraska at
Lincoln, F.M. Hall Collection

20   *Woman*, 1953
oil and charcoal on paper
mounted on canvas
25⅝ x 19⅝ inches
Hirshhorn Museum and
Sculpture Garden, Smithsonian
Institution, Gift of Joseph H.
Hirshhorn, 1966

22 *Woman*, 1954
oil on paper
20 x 14⅝ inches
Permanent Collection of the
Weatherspoon Art Gallery, The
University of North Carolina at
Greensboro; Charles and Laura
Dwan Memorial Gift

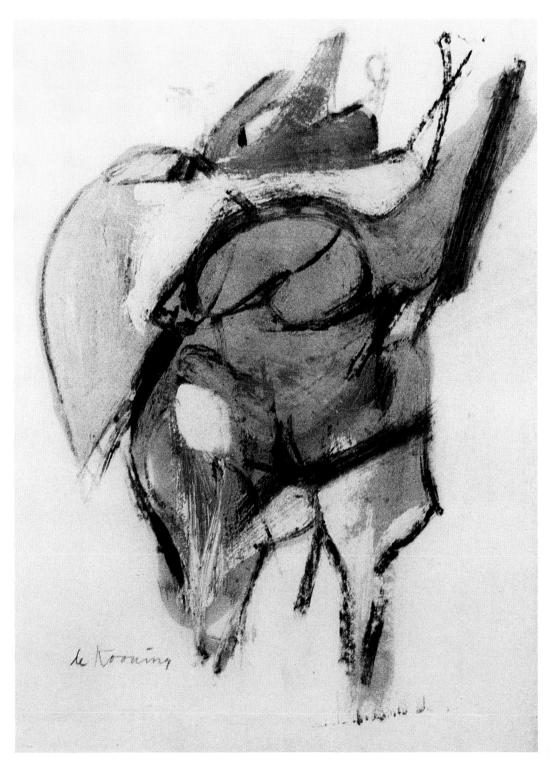

24 *Woman*, c. 1955
oil, enamel, charcoal on paper,
mounted on linen
28 x 20 inches
Collection Albright-Knox Art
Gallery; gift of Seymour H.
Knox, 1986

85

25   *Woman*, c. 1955
ink on paper
23½ x 18½ inches
Collection Luke Luyckx

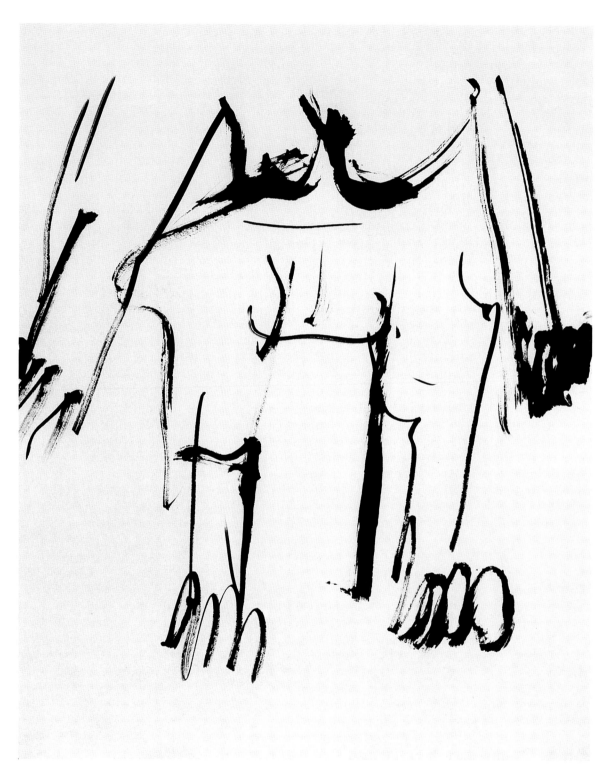

23 *Arrangement in Pink and
Green*, 1955
oil on cardboard
21½ x 25½ inches
Seattle Art Museum, Gift of
Mrs. Sidney Gerber and the
late Mr. Gerber

Robert Goodnough

Robert Goodnough is a senior member of the second generation of abstract expressionism. This generation responded creatively to the achievement of the first generation and especially the work of Jackson Pollock. Along with Goodnough, Helen Frankenthaler, Morris Louis, Kenneth Noland, and Friedel Dzubas were all producing significant work by the late 1950s.

From the first, Goodnough's work stood apart due to his insistence on relatively small scale, cubist drawing. But while he stuck to cubist line and shape, the size and handling of his pictures were abstract expressionist. Unlike the other members of his generation, he didn't turn to the "color-field" side of abstract expressionism until later in his career (in this he was like Robert Motherwell). Instead, he stuck with Pollock's emphasis on drawing.

Goodnough is also unique in that, until the middle sixties, he worked in both a purely abstract mode and in what must be called an abstract/figurative mode. The latter comes from Matisse and Picasso. Among the members of the first generation, only de Kooning and Pollock worked in both an abstract and an abstract/figurative mode. The mature works of all of the others were completely abstract. This is also true of all of the best painters of the second generation except for Fairfield Porter, who was completely representational.

Many if not most of Goodnough's best pictures of the early 1960s, perhaps his greatest period, are large scale, multiple figure works like *Devils in a Boat*. They achieve success where Picasso's *Guernica* and de Kooning's women fail. They are the only postwar, abstract/figurative works that compare to Pollock's *Portrait and a Dream* (at the same time they are not as radical in style as Pollock's picture, which is no longer cubist and does new things with scale).

Why did Goodnough give up the abstract/figurative mode after the early 1960s and concentrate completely on abstraction? Probably for the same reason that most of our best painters have concentrated completely on abstraction. The abstract painting invented by Pollock and his generation has turned out to be rich, self-sustaining and absorbing. The neo-expressionists try to revive the abstract/figurative mode, but they do so in a routine and uninspired way. Above all they can't *draw*. Here is where Goodnough has a lesson to teach us. ■

Kenworth W. Moffett

26 *Laocoön I*, 1958
oil on canvas
66⅜ x 54⅛ inches
The Museum of Modern Art,
New York, Given anonymously,
1959

28 *Abduction XI*, 1961
oil on canvas
72¼ x 84⅜ inches
National Museum of American
Art, Smithsonian Institution, Gift
of S.C. Johnson & Son, Inc.

29 *Devils in a Boat*, 1963
oil on canvas
84 x 84 inches
Courtesy Vivian Horan Fine Art

Grace Hartigan

"Symbols are my world. Such things as nudes, demons, gods, heroes, saints — This is all very well, now where to begin?" In 1952 Grace Hartigan scribbled this entry in her private journal. During the previous four years, Hartigan had executed her first mature paintings in an abstract expressionist mode. Yet by 1952 she restlessly felt the need to expand that means of expression. Instinctively, she began to teach herself the history of art and to discover what role expressive figuration might play in her paintings. Hartigan made frequent visits to The Metropolitan Museum of Art, often in the company of Larry Rivers and John Bernard Myers. Her interest in Western art history was not at all common among the abstract expressionist generation. As a whole those artists tended to avoid sources in the post-Renaissance tradition. More often they looked to non-Western and primitive art as inspiration.

During 1952 and 1953 Hartigan created eight free studies after Old Master art in which she widened both her iconographic and formal vocabulary. The first of these, *The Knight, Death and the Devil* (1952), was based on Albrecht Dürer's print of the same name. Dürer's small, highly detailed engraving of 1513, which symbolizes Christian fortitude, seems an odd choice as a starting point for Hartigan. Yet she was initially attracted by the subject matter, which she perceived romantically: "I imagined I was the knight embarking on a journey with these new paintings to who knew where." Indeed, the knight, painted glowing white in her picture, shines forth as a commanding presence and the epitome of adventure. The ragged edges of the paint patches pay homage to abstract expressionism and communicate movement, all in keeping with the theme of a journey undertaken.

The structure of Dürer's print also helped Hartigan, for while still wanting to emphasize the picture surface, she was interested in replacing the web of brushstrokes found in her earlier work with strong compositional massing. When Hartigan finished *The Knight, Death and the Devil*, she invited Rivers and Myers to the studio, where they admired it. Other associates were less supportive. The influential art critic Clement Greenberg told her to stop painting figurative canvases, and after she refused, they seldom spoke. Hartigan concluded, "I like [the painting] but fear I couldn't exhibit it. Very puzzled as to my motivations, but I must trust my instincts."

Hartigan's last, largest and most complex painting after the Old Masters is *River Bathers* (1953). In it she came full circle to modernism and Matisse, whose *Bathers by a River* (1916-17) she had studied at the 1951-52 Matisse retrospective at The Museum of Modern Art. Her canvas is not simply a tribute to the French master; it represents a sophisticated understanding of Matisse's motives and a reinterpretation of his painting.

Matisse's *Bathers by a River*, in which the cold, grey figures are trapped by a ruthless pictorial geometry, symbolizes a "vanishing paradise." Hartigan wrote in her journals of 1952, "Matisse is at his best, not when he is cozy, but when he puts you off." While Matisse's paradise disappears through sterilization, Hartigan disintegrates hers with brash physical energy. In *River Bathers*, her four schematic nudes are irregularly spaced across the canvas surface, and their poses reveal discomfort about their nudity. The figure to the far left side covers his genital area and the rotund nude in the upper right corner hangs his head. Hartigan has conceived their environment in terms of slashing brushstrokes which fly at breakneck speed toward all edges of the canvas. These jagged strokes which tear into one another suggest a discordant world where fast-paced images of sea, sand, grass and striped awnings all collide.

Hartigan's personal experiences with bathers occured at the crowded beaches near New York City, where she frequently took her son during the hot summers. There, where the beautiful and grotesque were juxtaposed, she discovered the awkwardness of modern urban man's near-nudity and interaction with nature. Modern life has no simple paradise. Hartigan's *River Bathers* is really an antipastoral work which expresses the excitement, provocativeness and awkwardness of physical, and perhaps psychological, nakedness in a contemporary context.

Grand Street Brides (1954) is Hartigan's *chef-d'oeuvre* of the fifties. In it she combined her interpretations of past art with her observations of street life (high culture and popular culture) and synthesized these into a powerful statement about modern alienation. Since 1949 Hartigan's studio had been in the Jewish quarter of the Lower East Side of Manhattan on Essex and Hester Streets. Nearby Grand Street, which featured rows of bridal shops, their windows filled with mannequins, provided a kind of everyman's art waiting to be transformed by the artist.

31 *River Bathers*, 1953
oil on canvas
69⅜ x 88¾ inches
Collection Museum of Modern
Art, New York, Given
anonymously, 1954

Hartigan recognized the wedding ritual as the most elaborate
ceremony commonly preserved into modern times. Yet it
seemed particularly ironic to her to watch the post-war generation rushing into marriage, seeking security, especially since
she had already been involved in two unfulfilling marriages.
At the same time that Hartigan was keenly observing contemporary existence, she was thinking of past art, particularly the
Spanish court scenes of Velazquez and Goya. As two fencers
might parry, she matched her own insights against theirs. *Grand
Street Brides* is particularly reminiscent of Goya's *Family of
Charles IV* (1800), in which the royal family is posed
awkwardly and overdressed and appears all the more clumsy
and isolated as a consequence.

Drawing on the past and the present, the overall mood of *Grand
Street Brides* is one of loneliness. There are no grooms in sight,
and the six brides, who suggest both mannequins and humans,
line up across the picture surface mutely appealing to the
viewer and unable to communicate with each other. The style of
the painting also contributes to its somber character. In the last
stages of the work, Hartigan rubbed down large areas of the
canvas with turpentine-soaked rags, as if she were searching for
the essence of personality beneath the elaborate costumes.
Just as she completed *Grand Street Brides*, Hartigan wrote to
her new friend, art critic Harold Rosenberg, "I think some of
my subjects are alienation, loneliness and anxiety. . . . The
figures in my paintings ask 'What are we doing? What do we
mean to each other?' They never look at each other, but have
some personal meaning."

The Vendor (1956), which Hartigan conceived in an entirely
different mood than the pensive *Grand Street Brides*, celebrates
the artist's vivacity, wit and compassion in the context of
modern urban life. The painting is a patchwork of broad color
planes. The vibrant colors relate to her frantic painting *River
Bathers*, though without its slashing brushwork. The glowing
white tonalities of *The Vendor* recall *The Knight, Death and the
Devil*, though they suggest physical joy more than spiritual
radiance.

32 *Grand Street Brides*, 1954
oil on canvas
72 x 102½ inches
Lent by the Whitney Museum
of American Art, New York;
Gift of an anonymous donor,
55.27

The Vendor was inspired by merchants with their pushcarts common throughout Hartigan's neighborhood. In the painting fragile cups, saucers and bowls are humorously recreated in teetering vertical piles balanced on a schematic pushcart. These details emphasize the two-dimensional picture surface as well as the artist's wit. On the right side of the painting, the tall and wild-eyed vendor is at once a comical and a commanding presence. Despite his funny facial features and costume of baggy pants and high black boots, he is painted in authoritative, angular brushstrokes and strong colors. As a willful and unusual personality, he commands his environment just as Hartigan commands her artistic means.

As one of Hartigan's "city life" paintings, *The Vendor* expresses another side of the artist's personality, her joy and hope. The characters, objects and sensations of the urban environment provided cause for celebration and contemplation of the human condition. The painting reflects a spontaneous optimism that is one aspect of the second generation of abstract expressionists and of America generally during the 1950s.

Grace Hartigan's recourse to figuration in the 1950s resulted from an intuitive desire to broaden her pictorial feelings. Using imagery from high culture, low culture and autobiography, she did not abandon, but rather amplified, the lessons in painterly abstraction she had absorbed from Pollock and de Kooning. One year after finishing *The Vendor*, Hartigan began her "place paintings," which though based upon her experiences of landscape, contain no recognizable objects.

Throughout her career Hartigan has been inspired simultaneously by abstract concepts and figurative sources in her art. Although critics and historians have often found it convenient to separate the two modes, she and other members of her generation found them complementary. Amid negative criticism of Philip Guston's return to figurative imagery, de Kooning once remarked, "What's the problem? This is all about freedom." ■

Robert Saltonstall Mattison

34 *Show Case*, 1955
oil on canvas
69¼ x 80¼ inches
The Metropolitan Museum of
Art, Roy R. and Marie S.
Neuberger Foundation, Inc.,
Fund, 1956 (56.199)

33 *The Masker*, 1954
oil on canvas
72 x 41 ¾ inches
Vassar College Art Gallery,
Poughkeepsie, New York,
Gallery Purchase, 54.9

35 *The Vendor*, 1956
oil on canvas
68 x 90 inches
Oklahoma Art Center, Museum
Purchase, Washington Gallery
of Modern Art

Lester Johnson

For Lester Johnson, the 1950s was a decade of exploration, as he shifted back and forth between abstraction and figuration in the process of determining the most direct way of expressing the substance of his art. He was to find his characteristic content in the emotional realities of urban life and to discover in expressionism his most eloquent stylistic vehicle. The twenty-eight-year-old painter arrived in New York from Minneapolis in 1947, having studied with Alexander Masley at the Minneapolis School of Art and with Cameron Booth at the St. Paul School of Art. From his teachers, who had both been students under Hans Hofmann in Germany, Johnson received a firm education in modernism, with an emphasis on the spatial implications of cubism. In the later forties, Johnson shared a Lower East Side studio with Larry Rivers. His work then consisted of small urban landscapes,[1] abstract landscapes, and geometric investigations of pure form.

Johnson's emergence as a figurative expressionist in the later fifties had come about in stages during the first half of the decade. In 1950 he stopped painting for a short while, having pushed his form "as far as it would go."[2] He was working afternoons as a framer for Baroness Hilla Rebay at the Guggenheim Museum, which was then housed in an old townhouse. Much of his time was spent in a depressing, low-ceilinged basement space. One day there he spontaneously began to draw an image of a dying plant, which "came from the heart, not the head" and which led him into the emotional content of form. In that year he exhibited as part of a group called 813 Broadway with Wolf Kahn, Felix Pasilis, Jan Müller and Miles Forst.

His first solo show at the Artists Gallery in 1951 included a variety of approaches, covering an early representational view, drawings of abstract landscapes and several thickly painted, "moody"[3] colored geometric abstractions with such resonant titles as *The Ironmaker* and *The Hero*. In his *Art News* review of the show, Robert Goodnough discussed the formal properties of the piled circles in *The Hero*, but missed, from Johnson's perspective, the psychological implications of the composition. Johnson's instinct for humanistic content was spurred by a second breakthrough incident that year. While working on a self-portrait, his frustration led him to wipe it all out and paint seven black diamonds on a green background. With a tube of black paint he then drew in seven faces, unconsciously creating a symbolic portrait of himself and his siblings. Although he still pursued both figurative and abstract means to his end, all his subsequent paintings had a psychological content. This was noted by critic Emily Genauer, who, in her review of Johnson's 1954 show of hard-edged, symbolic figurative works at the Korman Gallery, observed that he "communicates his profound, even mystical understanding of and sympathy for the jungle which is the human heart."[4]

For his 1955 exhibition at the Zabriskie Gallery, Johnson showed a series of tightly contoured single figures anchored in space by constricting loops of pure color. At about this time, Johnson became a member of the eminent Eighth Street Club of artists. He was to be the sole member of The Club to devote himself to figural paintings. Although he worked with an expressionist palette early in the decade, Johnson evolved into gestural expressionism only after 1956. His style became increasingly free, as the process of painting became more of a pleasurable, physical act. As the decade shifted into the sixties, Johnson's emotive content was embodied in his subjects, compositions and style: his canvases emphasized the primacy of the human figure essentially inhabiting the entire field of vision. Expressive, gestural brushstrokes and drips conveyed the unbridled energy of the process of painting. In *Three Heads* (1960), an intense, activated blue ground is a foil for three dark frontal figures, cut off by the frame on three sides.

37 *Broadway Street Scene*, 1962
oil on canvas
60¼ x 78¼ inches
National Museum of American
Art, Smithsonian Institution,
Gift of Mr. and Mrs. David K.
Anderson, Martha Jackson
Memorial Collection

Johnson has always been engaged by the activities of the street. His studios were normally just one flight up, affording a slightly distanced view of events below. Regarding *Broadway Street Scene* (1962), Johnson has written:

> I did this painting on Broadway and twenty-eighth Street. During the day there was always activity; import-export salesmen, toy distributors, etc. The luncheonettes were jammed at noontime. In my painting I was working for forms that were alive, that moved across the canvas, and never set, that had some of the noise, chaos and order of the city.[5]

The horizontal trail of activated feet making their way across the top of the picture seems like an off-register frame from a vertical strip of film. Multiple readings of this unusual device range from a literal interpretation of Johnson's interest in alive forms "that move across the canvas," to a motif derived from representations of the Ascension, where only the feet, calves and lower garments were depicted to convey that the figure had arisen.

The word "blue" floats across the surface of *Broadway Street Scene*, straying in front of the central head in one place and looping along the lower edge in another. From time to time Johnson augmented his paintings with color names, playing their graceful calligraphic curves against the vigorous, raw strokes with which he defined the human image. As a formal device, the cursive coils are not unrelated to the abstract spiral bands in his mid-fifties figure paintings. But here, by naming names, by presenting his color in both word and deed, Johnson also invokes a more literary tradition, as in poet Federico Garcia Lorca's impassioned revelation "Verde que te quiero verde" (Green, how much I want you green).

38 *Walking Men Green*, 1963
oil on canvas
80¼ x 59⅝ inches
National Museum of American
Art, Smithsonian Institution,
Gift of Mr. and Mrs. David K.
Anderson, Martha Jackson
Memorial Collection

A darker shower of pigment settles across the lower left section of *Portrait with Feet* (1963), veiling the distinction between figure and ground. The black-outlined subject and the field share the self-same surface plane of rapidly brushed ochre and green. *Portrait with Feet* erupts with a powerfully emotive content, as energetic spurts of pigment leap like sun flares beyond the limit of the head. Trailing drizzles of paint read as easily as tears as they do the signature technique of a master expressionist. As in *Broadway Street Scene*, Johnson thwarted the painting's strong frontal presence by brushing in a rhythmic file of feet at the upper edge.

Walking Men Green (1963) was one of the series of images of Bowery "bums" that Johnson initiated in his new Bowery St. studio: "I walk on the street on my way to my studio; the bums have beautiful faces. . . . I love them for their clothes, their baggy pants. God knows where they found their hats."[6] Johnson observed their street body language and was inspired by those animated moments when they embodied "the essence of physical freedom."[7] In *Walking Men Green* he balanced the constraints of their mean existence against a raw, robust vitality, conflating it with the very act of expressionist painting. ■

Judith Stein

Notes

1. Two of his gouaches, entitled *White Church* and *Chicago Landscape*, were included in the 1949 Pennsylvania Academy of the Fine Arts watercolor annual.

2. Lester Johnson, in conversation with the author and Paul Schimmel, February 3, 1988. All subsequent unattributed quotations are from this interview.

3. A contemporary description by Mary Cole, "Minneapolis Artist Has One-Man N.Y. Show," unidentified clipping in the collection of the artist.

4. E[mily]. G[enauer]., "Korman Shows Johnson," *New York Herald Tribune*, February 6, 1954.

5. Lester Johnson, *Contemporary Urban Visions* (New York: New School Art Center, 1966; exhibition catalog), p. 9.

6. Lester Johnson quoted in Lawrence Campbell, "Lester Johnson on the Bowery," *Art News* (February, 1964), p. 47.

7. Ibid., p. 60.

39 *Portrait With Feet*, 1963
oil on canvas
80 x 60 inches
Collection of the artist

Alex Katz

Figurative expressionists in the fifties generally stressed the process of painting, using it to discover their imagery. A few, notably Alex Katz, Fairfield Porter, Jane Freilicher, and for a time, Larry Rivers, emphasized subject. Katz was so intent on realism that he concentrated on portraits, the most specific of subjects, and he aimed to achieve accurate likenesses. He recognized that overlapping and scumbled, open brushwork obliterated details, getting in the way of representation, but he did not want to abandon it entirely—not yet. Instead, he tried to have it both ways, finding the edge between truth to appearances and painterly painting. What made Katz's problem even more difficult was his felt need to heighten his color, as Matisse had, and this required the suppression of rendering, modeling, and brushiness.

Katz's painterly painting was inspired by the prevailing avant-garde style, exemplified by the canvases of Willem de Kooning, Franz Kline, and Philip Guston, although it lacked the expressionist vehemence in vogue at the time. But the informal facture was also in character with Katz's sitters—his wife Ada, and artist, art world, poet, and dancer friends, "secret celebrities," as David Antin has called them.[1] The style of painting contributed to the realization of his subjects and their bohemian life styles.

This is particularly clear in Katz's picture of *Edith and Rudy (Burckhardt)* (1957). "Fugitives," as Katz called them in an article he wrote on Rudy, they are casual and plain but not "dirty-ankle[d]," a little down-in-the-mouth and stoop-shouldered, but nonetheless glamorous. Edith and Rudy look doggedly independent and self-sufficient; the gap between the figures is revealing. The outside world, the middle-class world—its paraphernalia and, by extension, its temptations and demands—is ignored, as it was in Burckhardt's life. A masterful photographer, film-maker, painter, and writer, he was "a Downtown Renaissance Man" and an "amateur," because his "art is not for money, not for careerism and is not an exclusive occupation."[2] Rudy's brother, then a supreme court justice in Switzerland, once told me that he believed Rudy was ashamed of his brother's worldly success.

Most of Katz's pictures are about the moment in which they were painted. In this sense, they are documentary. But a few suggest that they were remembered scenes, even implying a narrative. One such work is *Rockaway* (1961). In it, a sailor and a marine, all in grays, flank a pretty red-haired girl in a pink dress, each holding one of her hands. The scene calls to mind World War II and may even refer to Katz's own hitch in the Navy in 1945. The servicemen in sharp profile appear to be vying for the girl's attention, but in such a sober and reticent manner and with a gaze so rapt that they end up seeming to worship her. The picture takes on the hieratic aspect of an icon. The girl allows her hands to be held but pays her suitors no mind, instead looking directly at the viewers. She is indeed an alluring beauty, a kind of World War II Madonna, the pin-up of "the girl I left behind" and "who'd be so nice to come home to," to quote from nostalgic pop songs of the time. The figures seem to be out of the past, but Katz also insists on perceptual realism. The subjects are known art-world figures posing in costume, playing roles that Katz assigned to them. The image encompasses the reality of the present moment, that is, of the sitters being themselves in Katz's studio but acting out his story line, and their appearance is shaped both by what Katz is looking at and recalling while painting.

Ada Ada (1959) is the first of what Edwin Denby has called Katz's "reduplicative" portraits.[3] Portraying two Adas in the same space is an artifice, but it causes us to look at Ada's likeness twice. At the same time, it focuses attention on the subtle variations in painting from one Ada to the other. Thus, while doubling specific representation, Katz singles out the artifices of painting. Elsewhere, I have compared Katz's "reduplicative" portraits to Robert Rauschenberg's *Factum 1* and its near twin, *Factum 2* (1957), and it is noteworthy that Katz painted a double portrait of Rauschenberg. "An Expressionist painting is supposed to be *found* in the anxious struggle of painting, not *made*. By making the second *Factum* more or less indistinguishable from the first, Rauschenberg subverted the moral stance of gesture painting, an act of witty iconoclasm that delighted Katz."[4] But more than that, it underscored conscious intentionality and artistry, values Katz prized.

40 *Edith and Rudy*, 1957
oil on canvas
36 x 59⅝ inches
Courtesy Robert Miller Gallery

Figurative expressionism that verged too close to realism was suspect in the fifties. But Katz persisted not only because he wanted to paint portraits but because he recognized that there was a glut of gestural painting and thus that it was no longer a challenging style. More importantly, he had come to believe that figurative painting, if it were to become a major tendency, would have to be based on observed reality, and this would require the elimination of brushy facture. Furthermore, the size and scale of figurative paintings would have to be enlarged so that they would hold their own in visual impact and grandeur with the "big" abstract canvases that were commanding art world interest. And that was the course that Katz would take in the sixties. ■

Irving Sandler

Notes

1. David Antin, "Alex Katz and Tactics of Representation," in Irving Sandler and William Berkson, eds., *Alex Katz* (New York: Praeger, 1971), p. 16.

2. Alex Katz, "Rudolph Burckhardt: Multiple Fugitive," *Art News* 62 (December 1963), pp. 38-41.

3. Edwin Denby, "Katz: Collage, Cutout, Cutup," *Art News* 63 (January 1965),
p. 42.

4. Irving Sandler, *Alex Katz* (New York: Harry N. Abrams, 1979), p. 22.

42 *The Black Dress*, 1960
oil on canvas
71½ x 83½ inches
Courtesy Robert Miller Gallery

41 *Paul Taylor*, 1959
oil on canvas
66 x 73 inches
Courtesy Robert Miller Gallery

43 *Rockaway*, 1961
oil on canvas
83 x 72 inches
Courtesy Robert Miller Gallery

George McNeil

The four paintings by George McNeil in this exhibition are among his first figurative works and represent a critical juncture that has been of lasting importance in his long, flourishing career. They foretell the high color, movement, painterliness, and strong delineation in his work over the past two decades.

A student at the Hofmann School of Fine Arts from 1932 until 1936, McNeil credits Hofman with teaching him about space, about how to "have the color planes moving in and out — something I've always tried to keep."[1] He began the practice that he continued until 1980 of setting up a still life each fall — "the most drab kinds of things, pots, apples, drapes, seashells, paper in abstract shapes" — in the interest of "opening up space." His two-dimensional organizations on the canvas, he believes achieve a "substantive rather than a decorative abstraction," retaining a sense of matter and reality, because they are translations from this initial three-dimensional experience.

At the same time that McNeil was painting in a geometric cubist style, however, he felt pulled toward a very different, very expressionistic kind of art. From time to time it broke through, both in his abstract paintings of strong vertical images such as *Recumbent* (1954), which suggests affinities with Kline, and in a burst of exuberant figurative paintings of cafes and cabarets on a trip to Cuba in 1940. McNeil believes that being in New York City at the high point of the abstract expressionist movement — where he was exposed to the "ferment" in the air, the "freedom of Pollock and particularly of de Kooning" with his strident women — is what finally converted him into an expressionist painter. McNeil's subdued secondary colors brightened; he overcame his resistance to larger canvases (*Luciana* is 7′4″ high by 6′8″ wide); and he transferred his canvases from the easel to the floor, which allowed him to be "literally *in* the painting." Strong central configurations, like nuclei, appeared in his abstractions. At this time he instinctively sought out a drawing class, that given by Mercedes Matter, where, along with Philip Pearlstein and Philip Guston, he drew from the female model for five years. Thus the stage was set for the emergence of the figure in his own work.

Only after he had been doing so for a year or two did McNeil realize that he had been improvising figures. His first was *Invitation* (1957), in which a slender tadpole-like creature with a small head and long stemlike legs emerges unbidden from between the color planes of an abstract painting. Carrying a lighted candle from the dark left side of the canvas into the warm yellow region on the right, the figure is the harbinger of *Jezebel* (1960), *Astor* (1958), *Luciana* (1960), and *Augury* (1961). These early figurative works initiate what would prove to be McNeil's lifelong direction, that of abstraction becoming increasingly subordinated to an intensified figuration. Furthermore, the paintings set up the creative tension between form and freedom, between overall composition and the figure, that has been sustained in McNeil's work since 1957.

An increasing figuration can be observed even between the four McNeil paintings in this exhibition, if they are arranged in the order above. In *Jezebel*, the wide diagonal coalescence of shifting colors, which extends from the top to the bottom of the painting, is simultaneously a nascent figure and the rawest, most chaotic of the abstract shapes in the work. The dancing figure in *Astor* is more discernible, but McNeil restricts his outlining to a few intermittent black contours. The figure is enveloped by rounded shapes, as McNeil moves away from geometric abstraction. More roundnesses appear in the earthy woman who emerges in *Luciana*: the flower in her hair, her face, her breasts. Although completely identifiable as figure, *Luciana* is not a substantial entity; some parts of the figure are traced in white over abstract forms that exist independently of it; other parts are floating, unenclosed color, with the gestural field still very much clinging to the figure. In *Augury*, however, McNeil deliberately "implores, grasps, and outlines" the improvised figure as it emerges from the inteplay of lines, shapes, and colors — a practice that he would follow with increasing intensity in the years to come. *Augury* is the most delineated of McNeil's four paintings in this exhibition. The figure's face is outlined in white, and her shoulders, back, and buttocks are drawn with ochre paint in a sinuous S-shape that divides the canvas into four abstract planes.

44 *Astor*, 1958
oil on canvas
66 x 66 inches
Lent by the Whitney Museum
of American Art, New York;
Purchase, with funds from an
anonymous donor. 59.17

Bringing in the human figure, McNeil discovered, extended the expressiveness of his abstraction. With the figure, he says, he could "get down to the very basic drives of sexuality and fantasy." In these early figures, graphic outline and expressions of the human condition were not as important to McNeil as were energy, directional movements of form and brushstroke, and color. McNeil has described them as "mainly painting vehicles" to convey the "sensate, the Dionysian." The figure in *Augury* is the least attached of the four to its gestural field and so is the freest to dance. Not touching down, she is a tug of oppositions—her legs kicking in opposite directions, her arms going one way, her streaming scarves the other. Color heightens within the four paintings; central parts of the figures in *Luciana* and *Augury* are a rich grape color, which vibrates against other zones of royal blue, cadmium red or yellow, and orange.

For McNeil the figure must never disrupt the total organization of the painting; in other words, the creative tension between figure and composition must be maintained. Even as he delineates, he practices what he calls "hidden abstraction" by making color planes work independently of the figure. Rather than seeing the figure as a statue, a phenomenon in space, he views it more ambiguously, as an abstract, two-dimensional element. Instead of breaking up the surface of his paintings, the figure becomes an extension or embodiment of form, form being the canvas as a compositional whole. "I want things to go apart and then to hold," McNeil explains. "The concept of resolution is very deep within me. It's like a conscience." ∎

Judith Higgins

Notes

1. Quoted comments were made by George McNeil during six interviews with the author in 1986, for a profile in *Art News*, and during an interview in May 1988 for this essay.

45 *Luciana*, 1960
oil on canvas
88 x 80 inches
Collection of the artist,
Courtesy M. Knoedler & Co.

46   *Jezebel*, 1960
oil on canvas
88 x 80 inches
Collection Walker Art Center,
Minneapolis; Gift of the T.B.
Walker Foundation, 1962

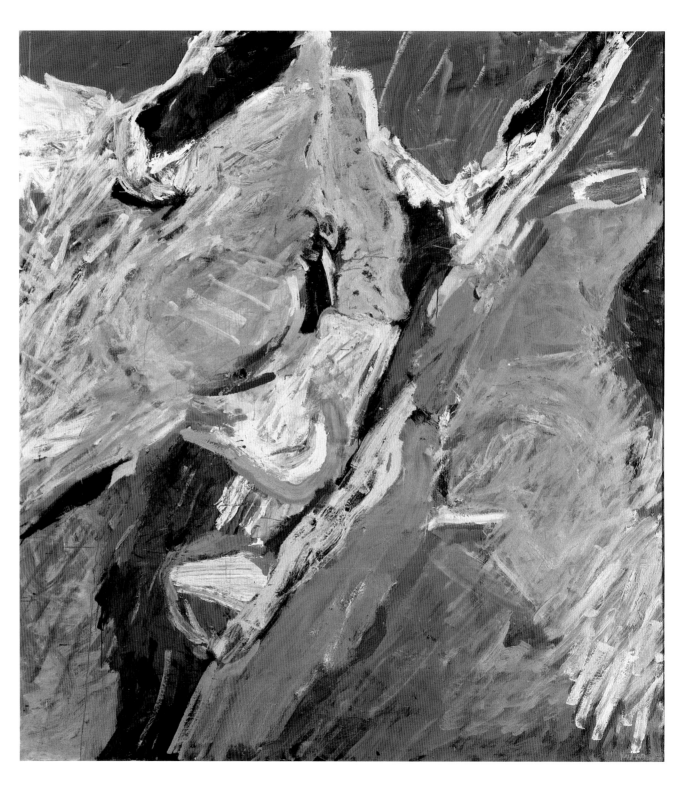

47 *Augury*, 1961
oil on canvas
78 x 84 inches
Collection of the artist,
Courtesy M. Knoedler & Co.

Jan Müller

Jan Müller was born in Hamburg, Germany in 1922. From the time Hitler came to power in 1933, until 1941, when Müller came to the United States, he and his family were on the move across Europe. He lived for short periods of time in Prague, in rural Switzerland and in Amsterdam. In Lyon, France in 1940 he was interned as a German refugee in a prison camp. Released after the French signed their armistice with Germany, he moved south. He would later recapture the light and palette of southern France in his lush landscapes, with and without figures, and in the mysterious "path" paintings, inspired also by his visits to Provincetown, Massachusetts. He pushed ahead through Spain to Lisbon, from where he eventually journeyed, with only part of his family, to America. At the age of thirty-six the rheumatic fever that had begun to drain his strength and damage his heart on the pilgrimage across Europe finally claimed his life. He died in New York City in 1958.

Many who knew him and his work have paid tribute to Müller, each in his or her own way. Friends speak caringly of him. Dody Müller has given us a vivid account of her husband's life for the catalog of the 1962 retrospective of his work at The Guggenheim Museum. Thomas Messer, former director of The Guggenheim, organized the exhibition and also contributed an essay to its catalog. Martica Sawin, in her *Arts Magazine* article of 1959, has provided a broad and very insightful study of Müller's life and work, with a concern for both the style and iconography of his paintings. Meyer Schapiro wrote a characteristically sensitive remembrance of Müller in a catalog for the 1962 Venice Biennale; and Richard Bellamy, former director of the Hansa Gallery, of which Müller was a central figure, assembled in 1985 a beautiful exhibition of the artist's late paintings at the Oil and Steel Gallery in lower Manhattan. Artists such as Mary Frank continue to evoke in their own work the impressive accomplishment of their ill-fated friend and fellow artist Jan Müller.

From 1945 to 1950 Müller studied with Hans Hofmann. In this period he developed a style of abstract mosaic painting with strong ties to the color harmonies of Klee. In these early works Müller embraced that single unit of design, the square—either oddly or perfectly shaped—that fascinated the Bauhaus faculty and their progeny. Müller's abstract mosaic fields, highly compressed and often restless, go beyond their simple, ordinarily repetitive means. Occasionally organized in meaningful formats and combinations such as cruciform compositions, these early works strain to express themselves. In time, Müller would give them a chance to do so.

Mondrian's career came to an end while he was most deeply preoccupied with the quasi-molecular behavior of the tiny square and its identification with the beat of modern urban life. Reinhardt went on, beyond the impressionist-pointillist-cubist heritage embodied in that same gene, the little square, to a nearly ruthless subtraction from the standard elements of style in order to achieve sublimity in painting. And Hofmann, of course, sought to resolve the conflict between geometry and emotion, striking a balance in his "slab" paintings between the mighty right angle and expressive brushwork. Müller, younger by far than the established figures of the New York School, turned in 1954 from his abstract mosaics of greens, reds, yellows and blues to mosaics of nature and figures encircled and linked to each other by fields of energy. The dense environments in his last paintings stand as worlds unto themselves, like the broad fields and cosmic landscapes of Van Gogh.

48 *Bacchanale in Sunlight*, 1956
oil on canvas
49⅛ x 96 inches
Solomon R. Guggenheim
Museum, New York, Gift, Mr.
and Mrs. Donald Erenberg, 1985

Müller's most memorable works were all painted in the last four years of his life, at a time when he knew he did not have long to live.

We do not know for sure what circumstances or changes in thinking brought about this shift in Müller's art from the abstraction of his mosaic paintings to the strongly figurative, more talkative and literary work that he made from 1954 to 1958. By 1954 it was clear to artists living in the New York area that Rothko and Kline represented one direction available to the younger generation of painters: that of abstract painting dedicated to the expressive capacities of abstract means. However, theirs was not the only way to go.

Paintings by Pollock from the fifties appear to reverse, or at least to modify, the degree of abstraction of the "drip" paintings with references back to the earlier archetypal imagery of the forties from which he had first emerged. Hofmann's paintings of the fifties continue to depict still lifes and interiors that unabashedly establish their ties to older European art. And, of course, de Kooning provided in his inhabited landscapes a strong role model for the younger painter seeking to reconcile expressive figuration and formal abstraction.

In their own time painters like Müller were not always sharply distinguished from the older generation; they were simply referred to as a "second generation" of the New York School. In 1957, when Leo Steinberg wrote about Müller and twenty-two other artists in *The New York School: Second Generation*, the catalog for an exhibition at The Jewish Museum, he recognized that these artists had "inherited," as he put it, most of the general aspects of the older generation.[1] Steinberg found their work, which he likened to the paintings of the older generation, "systematically uncouth." He identified other similarities as well: their abstraction, their appeal to the few, their unfinished surfaces, and the elusive significance of their images. In his essay Steinberg does not distinguish between artists whose work included figures and those whose did not, thus acknowledging the tendency for both modes in the work of the older generation as well.

Can we, then, so easily segregate artists like Müller from the older abstract expressionists of their time? Is it so clear that painters like Müller intended their works to be controversial statements—reactions against a severity and absolutism of abstraction practiced by the old generation of painters?

In 1954 a plastic valve was placed in Müller's damaged heart. His heartbeat became, like a time bomb, publicly audible, and the regular rhythms of his abstract mosaics gave way to the more energetic and disturbing existentialist subjects of his last works. Mosaic patterns, formerly patchwork-like, began to swerve and swirl in concert with active, often turbulent figures. Horizonless landscapes and no-way-out forests suggest extremes of closure and protection. Contests of angels and demons, constructed from Müller's knowledge of the Faust legends and his love for the multipanelled religious narratives of the German Middle Ages, suggest the artist's personal communion with the forces of good and evil in his last years. Pleasure and pain, bacchanal and witches' sabbath exist side by side in these last efforts by Müller to hurriedly complete his epic drama, at once both death-defying and relenting. ■

Jeffrey Hoffeld

Notes

1. Leo Steinberg, "Introduction," *The New York School: Second Generation* (New York: The Jewish Museum, 1957), pp. 4-8.

120

49   *Of This Time - Of That
Place*, 1956
oil on canvas
49½ x 95¾ inches
Collection Mr. and Mrs. John
Martin Shea

51 *Walpurgisnacht Faust II*,
1956
oil on canvas
82 x 102½ inches
Collection Howard and Barbara
Wise

50 *Faust I*, 1956
oil on canvas
68⅛ x 120 inches
Collection The Museum of
Modern Art, New York,
Purchase, 1957

54 *The Accusation*, 1957
oil on canvas
48 x 50 inches
Private Collection

52 *The Search for the*
Unicorn, 1957
oil on canvas
70⅛ x 93⅛ inches
Collection Alfred and Sondra
Ordover

53 *The Temptation of St.*
Anthony, 1957
oil on canvas
81 x 121 ½ inches
Lent by the Whitney Museum
of American Art, New York;
Purchase. 72.30

55 *Jacob's Ladder*, 1958
oil on canvas
83½ x 115 inches
Solomon R. Guggenheim
Museum, New York

Jackson Pollock

In *The Integration of the Personality*, published in English in 1939 when Pollock began his four-year Jungian analysis, Jung emphasized the importance of the image in the healing and centering process of individuation. "The symbolic process is an experience in the image and of the image . . . possible only when one allows the ego-consciousness to enter the image . . . that is, when no obstruction is offered to the happening of the unconscious."[1] What we might call an iconic approach to the image, in which psyche and image are one and the same, was crucial to Pollock's approach to art from the early 1940s until the end of his life.[2] In 1956 Pollock declared, "When you're painting out of your unconscious, figures are bound to emerge. We're all of us influenced by Freud, I guess. I've been a Jungian a long time."[3] The iconic image is characteristic not only of Jungian metaphysics but of much that influenced Pollock: the mysticism of his first art teacher in California, the animism of American Indian art, oriental psychological culture, the hermeticism of John Graham and the surrealist painters. Pollock's particular genius was to apply the iconic approach to modernist pictorial experimentation. He projected his growing understanding of the dynamism of opposites, derived from psychological culture and explored through his images, onto the pictorial surface and translated the structure of this dynamism into increasingly abstract paintings culminating in the poured abstractions of 1947-50.

The many-breasted figure in *Number 5* (1952) echoes the emphatically breasted figures that dominate his art circa 1942 — e.g., *Moon Woman, Stenographic Figure*, and *Male and Female*. Earlier this image signaled the fertility of Pollock's muse as she became aware of the creative play of opposites. Now she signals artistic crisis, after the synthesis achieved in the poured paintings has unraveled. The figure in *Number 5* is not only a goddess of fertility but a dark goddess with the capacity to destroy as well as to create. The full force of her threat is evident in her kinship with Pollock's earliest images of a destructive female, such as *Woman* (c. 1930-33).

Even in the midst of questioning the Jungian belief that the iconic image could center and heal him, Pollock continues to extend the implications of the iconic approach to formal experimentation. Building on the structural dynamic at the core of his art, he translates his intuitive understanding of the relationship of opposites into yet another new technique of sinking the poured black paint into the white ground or matrix of the raw canvas. He weds in a dynamic fusion black and white, figure and ground, movement and stasis. The oneness of psyche, image, and material means remains intact — up to the very edge of despair. ∎

Elizabeth Langhorne

Notes

1. C.G. Jung, *The Integration of the Personality* (New York: Farrar and Rinehart, 1939), pp. 89-90.

2. For a definition of icon see Ann Gibson, "The Rhetoric of Abstract Expressionism," in *Abstract Expressionism: The Critical Developments* (New York: Abrams, 1987), pp. 77-78.

3. Document 113, in F.V. O'Connor and E.V. Thaw, *Jackson Pollock: A Catalogue Raisonné of Paintings, Drawings and Other Works* (New Haven: Yale University Press, 1978), p. 275.

56 *Number 5*, 1952
enamel on canvas
56 x 31½ inches
Collection Modern Art
Museum of Fort Worth,
Purchase made possible by a
grant from the Anne Burnett
and Charles Tandy Foundation

Fairfield Porter

Few artists call up a milieu with such ease as Fairfield Porter, but the ease is deceptive. For the paintings' sunlight – and what sunlight! – covers (like darkness) numerous contradictions. In Porter's indian summer of impressionism on Long Island and Maine, the sea smiles, the sky is blue, houses are white, the wind – a yachtsman's wind – cuts across landscapes that wear their figures as casually as the figures wear their clothes. The vision appears to be one of haute bourgeois summering (sockless, except for children and tennis players) in clothes that have the good taste to be nondescript, to be merely colored.

Around these casual snapshots – things seen as if in a blink of sunlight – is a consoling sense of social order, of habit regularly certifying the stability of things, as it does in well-to-do childhoods. Problems seem as remote from this world as they were from that of the Gerald Murphys, who refused to let life interfere with living. Here things call out their names in litanies: boats, dogs, tabletops, jugs, fruits, cars grazing on grass, open milk cartons, furniture that though clumsy and unfashionable survives to serve summer needs and becomes invisible, porches, windows and, through windows, views blocked with verdure, which often give way to the sea, reflecting the sun in various disguises. And outdoors, a pleasure so intense it must be dissembled, for what is spoken of here is something that must be whispered from behind the hand: the praises of the failed god, Nature.

Is it this discretion that gives the work, for all its generosity, its reserve, even a kind of opacity? For this art had every reason to be shy of itself, presenting nature as a privileged sanctuary from within a group of abstract expressionists who were the artist's friends and, remarkably, his admirers. De Kooning and Porter had a strong mutual regard, and its superficial reflex can be read in some of their painterly handwriting. Around 1960, de Kooning's abstractions hunt a lost landscape which Porter sometimes seems to realize for him. Both, for different reasons, share modernism's terminal anxiety, which is connected with prohibitions and responsibilities. Most of Porter's landscapes are figureless. His studies of figures seem to me uncomfortable, and his painting them as if they were not does not soothe them. The portraits promise social and painterly graces which they do not fulfill. If ultimately there is a tentative figure in Porter's work, it is the artist himself, for his persona is distant and elusive. The ghost that paints the picture absents itself to the degree that its strategies are realized. In Porter's case, this ghost inhabits a residue of conflicts not easily resolved. This is not negative, for it admits of more problems than do paintings that bear off their successes more easily.

"The only way to regard his painting is as though here painting begins again." This is Porter writing of John Button's work, but the comment applies more to Porter's. One of the most educated of American artists, Porter was far more conversant with American traditions in painting than his colleagues. The sense of difficulty, which became almost canonical in the practice of abstract expressionism, may be associated with this idea of beginning again. But beginning again – mistrusting received information – is a characteristic of the best American painting in the nineteenth century. Porter was more equipped than his colleagues to perceive the connections – or disconnections – between past and present in the American tradition. That tradition is one of hesitations, determined empiricism, puzzled rationalizations and a reluctance to interfere with the way the world presents itself – all characteristics of Porter's paintings. Nature's sloppy autonomy reforms the artist's conventions; in the nineteenth century, Asher Brown Durand's sketches are exemplary. What is there is there. As Porter put it in an interview, "The rag on the floor was there and I liked it." In *A Short*

57 *Self-Portrait in the Studio*,
c. 1950
oil on canvas
45 x 30 inches
The Parrish Art Museum,
Southampton, New York, Gift
of the Estate of Fairfield Porter

Walk, what does that odd piece of color half-hidden by the right foreground tree represent? A dog? A jacket? A chair? Porter composes by letting nature compose itself, which strains his conventions so that "here painting begins again."

Under these responsibilities, Porter's art could lapse into primitive postures that are startling when one comes across them (e.g., *Nyack*). These moments are fascinating, for they represent the loss of nature, which is replaced by an awkard idea of it. The mind proceeds to contradict the eye, as if the artist, in a sudden panic, was forced to admit "My God, I've no idea how to paint at all!" This primitivism, again shared with some of the best nineteenth-century landscape painters, is revelatory. It certifies the artistic conscience at work, ever seeking to renew itself; it shows how insecure is the artist's hold on the pictorial codes he has evolved (particularly shape versus stroke, line versus color, often resulting in sudden lurches between plane and depth); and it gives one an eye to seek out, even in successful pictures, details where the outline of an idea edits those pulsations of color that assemble a scene with glorious clarity and freshness. Of all his paintings, *July Interior* is strange in these ways.

The foreground inventory from left to right reads magazine(?), glasses, book, face, sewing box, telephone, book. All are generalized except for the face and sewing box, which counterpose their specifics. But the face, however abstracted its gaze, sucks in our attention, for it particularizes in a set of things more generally seen. In the background, clock, mirror and books are delineated more as concepts. Nothing is as general as the mood of the landscape seen through the window. The outrageous red stripes of the cloth on the table augment the sewing box in diverting our attention from the face. A formal matter—the red—is introduced to modify a psychological weight—the face. In modernism, such dialectics were consciously implicit in the artist's method. In this picture, the uneasy congress of the specific and the general generate a variety of ambiguities which deepen when examined. Here the subject rides on different modalities of vision and representation as they strive toward consistency to fulfill the illusion of style as late modernism conceived it. It is the artist's awareness of these conflicts that certifies *July Interior* as a modern picture.

58 *Laurance Typing*, 1952
oil on canvas
40 x 30⅛ inches
The Parrish Art Museum,
Southampton, New York, Gift
of the Estate of Fairfield Porter

Porter's difficulties, like Milton Avery's, show most clearly in the portraits, which hesitate to engage the sitters deeply. The personal is sweated out of them, and intimacy subsumed in a general diffidence. The artist is helping the model hide. In the earlier portraits, a particular face crystalizes, doubtfully seeking consonance with the general mood. In later portraits, the struggle between type and individual is more muted. The only time I met Porter (indoors), the two of us were alone. Later it was difficult to recall his features, but his presence remained clear, like a shadow on a porch screen. His *Self-Portrait in the Studio* maintains that presence while withdrawing specifics. The author acknowledges himself, but more as medium than creator. This modesty, almost a form of good breeding, has served Porter's work very well. For it is the doorway to the outdoors where he painted some of the most splendid modern landscapes, in which nature, unpolluted by metaphor or grim topographies, is allowed to reinvent itself. ■

Brian O'Doherty

59 *Laurance at the Piano*, 1953
oil on canvas
40 x 30 inches
Courtesy Hirschl & Adler Modern

60 *Katie in an Armchair*,
1954
oil on canvas
65½ x 46 inches
Collection Katherine Porter

62 *Katie and Anne*, 1955
oil on canvas
80⅛ x 62⅛ inches
Collection Hirshhorn Museum
and Sculpture Garden,
Smithsonian Institution. Gift of
Joseph H. Hirshhorn, 1966

61 *Portrait of James Schuyler*,
1955
oil on canvas
48 x 42 inches
Collection Ashby McCulloch
Sutherland

66   *Lizzie at the Table*, 1958
oil on canvas
37 x 45 inches
Collection Arthur M. Bullowa

63 *Frank O'Hara*, 1957
oil on canvas
63⅞ x 45⅞ inches
Collection The Toledo Museum
of Art; Gift of Edward
Drummond Libbey

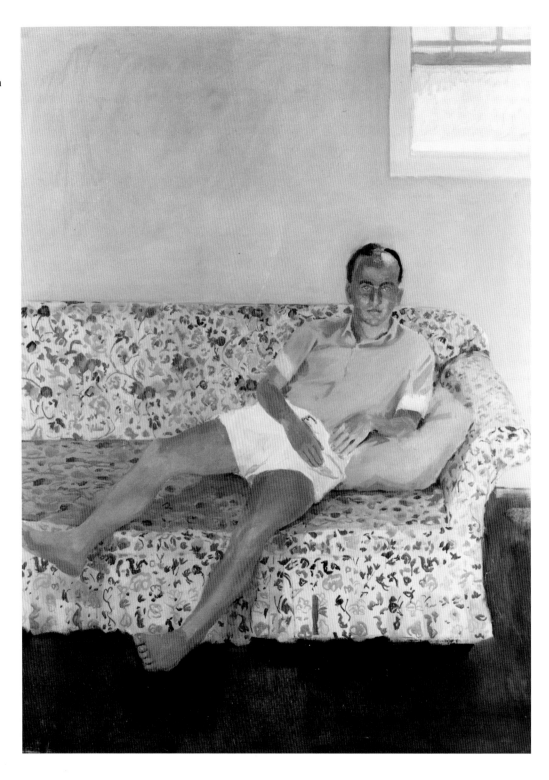

65   *Anne, Lizzie and Katie*, 1958
oil on canvas
78 x 60 inches
Nebraska Art Association,
Thomas C. Woods Memorial
Collection, Courtesy Sheldon
Memorial Art Gallery, Univer-
sity of Nebraska at Lincoln

Larry Rivers

Larry Rivers came to artistic maturity in an atmosphere of high creative energy, a condition to which his own internal dynamo was naturally geared to respond. Nervous, volatile and fiercely ambitious, determined to carve out an art world niche illuminated by its own limelight (and not the afterglow of abstract expressionism), he quickly moved from an early phase of Bonnard-inspired postimpressionism to a more radical brand of figurative modernism. His colors, once sunny and luminous, became dark, angry and opaque; his brushwork took on a furious animation; and his forms mutated from voluptuous calm to the aggressive agitation more suited to his temperament. In learning to trust his instincts, he set himself on the path to developing a solid foundation on which his art could rest.

The constant feature in this evolutionary process was the figure, a subject that has remained central to Rivers's art throughout his career. But unlike conventional portraits or studies of the human form, his figures are both embodiments of vitality and vehicles for interpreting that vital essence in plastic terms. Like others of his generation, his approach to pictorial problems was conditioned by his training with Hans Hofmann and exposure to achievements of the New York School, but he was nevertheless resolved to reconciling these modernist attitudes with his deep-seated need to derive stimulation from the observable world. And, at this stage in his development, it was his immediate circle of family and friends that stimulated him most effectively. Trusting his instincts meant freeing the figure from the customary constraints painting imposes. Instead of pinning it like a butterfly in a specimen case, he encouraged the figure to escape, to remain as vivacious and elusive as it is in life.

Loosening up his technique, as he did in *Two Women Posing* and other canvases of 1951-52 that reflect his debt to both Soutine and de Kooning, was merely the first step in this process. In fact, this phase proved to be a dead end, and for six months, Rivers made no paintings, concentrating instead on a series of figurative sculptures modeled in a hybrid mixture of plaster, cement and sand. In retrospect, this period of work in the round seems a retreat from the dissolution of form in his paintings of the early fifties—an affirmation of substance to counter a tendency toward fragmentation that he apparently mistrusted. Yet, with his move from New York City to Southampton, Long Island, in the spring of 1953, and while continuing his experiments in sculpture, Rivers began the series of canvases in which fragmentation was refined to a mature painting style. This may have been a case of the pendulum swinging back from the extreme solidity and stasis of the sculptures, which helped him work out more tangible problems of form until their possiblities were, for the time being, exhausted. At this point he was again ready to face the challenge of the figure on a two-dimensional plane, where the issue of representation was, by the mid-twentieth century, no longer a matter of likeness or anatomical accuracy.

Immediately it became apparent that Rivers was striving to represent not human beings but states of being human. Both the artist and his subjects were the cast of characters in an ongoing, open-ended drama of interaction, set on the stage of shared experience. In a penetrating observation made at this time, the painter and critic Fairfield Porter, a personal friend and fellow Southampton resident, wrote:

> If it is like an actor not to know who he is, then like an actor, and because he likes to experiment, Rivers acts out his life in search for a sound basis. It is as if all events in which he participates were crucial moments in his autobiography.[1]

For Rivers, in whose psyche art and life are inextricably linked, this "search for a sound basis" was carried on simultaneously in both realms. It was, in essence, a search for self.

67 *Two Women Posing*, 1952
oil on canvas
32½ x 53 inches
Collection of the artist

Rivers learned to value his instincts and to communicate them unequivocally, even if they were in themselves equivocal. The apparitional quality of figures half seen and half imagined, expressed as transitory beings, describes a pictorial equivalent of motion through shifting multiple poses, as in *Self-Figure* and *The Studio*, reflecting the restlessness of both Rivers's nature and his private life. On a deeper level, however, it speaks of something more universal: the temporal character of personal relationships. People move in space, but they also change with time — they come and go, in and out of the picture, in and out of one's life. The artist can fix them forever, but to Rivers, that would be dishonest, a denial of the thrill of discovery and fear of loss that underlie the anticipation of their entrances and exits.

The Studio is a composition bracketed by loss, poignantly commemorating two people who contributed in different ways but perhaps in equal measure to Rivers's creative coming of age. At the center is an anonymous black dancer, flanked by multiple nudes of Rivers's son Steven on the right and his step-son Joseph's clothed figure on the left, brandishing a banner proclaiming "liberty," a device that symbolizes the artist's emancipation from earlier influences and proclaims his esthetic independence. On either side, his mother-in-law Bertha (Berdie) Burger and his close friend, the poet Frank O'Hara, guard this hard-won liberty, the one with patient stoicism and the other as an alert sentinel. Within a year, Berdie would be dead, and O'Hara was to become the victim of a fatal accident a decade later. Looking now at their delicate, insubstantial figures — each viewed twice, as if a single aspect could not do them justice — we see them already as ghosts, less physical than spiritual, expressions of a subjective reality generated by emotional allegiance.

The multiple image was also a means of injecting narrative overtones, enhancing a picture's dramatic potential. The freeze-frame montage of arrested gestures in *Self-Figure* illustrates the artist's advance toward and retreat from his canvas, depicting creation as an activity, a collection of moments, a process of uncertain duration beginning before the inception of the

68 *Self-Figure*, 1953
oil and charcoal on canvas
93⅜ x 65½ inches
In the Collection of The
Corcoran Gallery of Art,
Museum Purchase, William A.
Clark Fund, 1955

finished product and continuing beyond its completion. In more concrete terms, this is also true of *Double Portrait of Berdie*, for which the docile and compliant Mrs. Burger posed nude in her Southampton bedroom. There is the implication that, over the course of time, she became bored with sitting and walked to the end of the bed, or that she tired of standing and sat down to rest—but further, that she entered the room and undressed before posing, and that she will dress again and leave it in due course. The progress of daily life and the artist's interpretive process have merged; art and life are one.

This painting charts a middle course between Rivers's translucent, fragmentary technique in such works as *The Studio, Self-Figure* and *July* and his so-called academic digressions, in which the figure is fully modeled and multiple views are eliminated. Rivers once described these exercises of the mid-fifties, which include the nude portraits of his estranged wife Augusta and of O'Hara, based on studies by the Romantic masters Delacroix and Géricault, respectively, as "either an attempt to be an Old Master, or to say, I don't know if this is art, but I want to do it."[2] In some ways echoing his earlier plaster sculpture, which he characterized as a means of dealing with physical reality in nonpainterly terms,[3] they affirm his search for substance by methodical scrutiny, a deliberate means of retarding his mercurial attachment to the transient.

By the decade's end, Rivers had proved that he needed no self-imposed restraints on his quicksilver tendencies. In the late fifties, having returned to his Manhattan loft, he evolved a more abstract syle, synthesizing aspects of his earlier phases: rich, gestural brushwork; luscious surfaces; montage compositions peppered with imagery interspersed with blank areas to be filled in by the viewer's imagination; along with a renewed interest in secondary source material in the form of snapshots and printed imagery. His preoccupations were allowed to develop into obsessions, generating series on the themes of life—especially happenstance, everyday occurrences, personal nostalgia and autobiography—and death, embodied in elderly and deceased Civil War veterans as pictured in *LIFE* magazine. Bold, energetically applied color (its vitality an antidote to the immobility of the subjects) unifies figure and ground into an overall pictorial field, with sketchy linear accents hinting at the details of facial features and body parts. This is as close as Rivers would ever come to pure abstraction.

71 *Double Portrait of Berdie*,
1955
oil on canvas
70¾ x 82½ inches
Collection Whitney Museum of
American Art, New York; Gift
of an anonymous donor, 56.9

Larry Rivers's Figurative Sculpture at the Stable Gallery, New York, 1954

Notes

1. Fairfield Porter, "Rivers Paints a Picture," *Art News*, January 1954, p. 57.

2. Quoted in Helen A. Harrison, "Look Ma, I'm Dancin'," *Larry Rivers: Peforming for the Family* (East Hampton, New York: Guild Hall Museum exh. cat., 1983), p. 6.

3. As paraphrased by Porter in "Rivers Paints a Picture," p. 58.

4. Frank O'Hara, "Larry Rivers: The Next to Last Confederate Soldier," in B. H. Friedman, ed., *School of New York: Some Younger Artists* (New York: Grove Press, 1959), p. 65.

However far removed from orthodox realism, these works retain their foothold in reality, or rather in experience, which is so often at odds with objective truth. Writing of one painting in this series, Frank O'Hara noted that

> *The Soldier's* fluctuation between figurative absence and abstract presence comes from an adamant attachment to substance, which is its source of energy. That is all, no identity. In his work Rivers is playing out, at whatever cost to himself, the drama of our lack.[4]

The figures' iconic, anonymous status, rather than their personalities, is emphasized; they become surrogates for artist and viewer alike. How else but through the figure could this anxiety be dramatized?

In all his stylistic diversions, Rivers was never to abandon the figure, which continues to be his primary motif. His quest for a sound basis has hinged upon the human factor, the common denominator that enables us to forge a psychic bond with even the most sketchily rendered image. The fact that, in his paintings of the fifties, the bond is often tenuous and elusive only makes us strive all the harder to establish it. ■

Helen A. Harrison

69   *Berdie in a Red Shawl*, 1953
oil on canvas
53 x 65 inches
Collection Whitney Museum of
American Art; Lawrence H.
Bloedel Bequest 77.1.44

70 *Portrait of Frank O'Hara*,
1954
oil on canvas
97 x 53 inches
Collection of the artist

72 *The Studio*, 1956
oil on canvas
82½ x 193½ inches
Lent by The Minneapolis
Institute of Arts; The John R.
Van Derlip Fund

73 *July*, 1956
oil on canvas
83 ¼ x 90 ¼ inches
Collection The Brooklyn
Museum, Anonymous Gift
(56.160)

75 *The Last Civil War*
Veteran, 1959
oil and charcoal on canvas
82½ x 64⅛ inches
The Museum of Modern Art,
New York, Blanchette
Rockefeller Fund, 1962

Bob Thompson

Bob Thompson's stylistic development roughly corresponds to the major chapters of his professional life. His early work coincides with his stay in New York from spring 1959 to spring 1961. During this time he executed a number of small oils on wood panels of various shapes, as well as works on canvas. Aside from an occasional self-portrait or portraits of his wife and friends, all of these paintings featured a brilliant, non-naturalistic palette and fictional scenes.

Prominent in many of these compositions is a dark, black or brown, silhouetted man in a broad-brimmed hat who seems to double as the artist and one of the giants of jazz music he loved.[1] In some instances, the man in the broad-brimmed hat acts as a *repoussoir*, directing the viewer from the periphery to the center of the canvas and indicating the artist's knowledge of baroque compositional devices.[2] But the silhouetted figure also joins with Thompson's schematic, candy-colored landscapes and faceless, pink-fleshed nude women to reveal his debt to the iconography of Jan Müller.

Thompson's art differs substantially from Müller's, however. The younger artist's palette tends to be hotter and his use of color generally violates the Hofmannesque balance of chromatic tensions seen in Müller. The sensuous contours that characterize Thompson's later treatment of the human figure are largely absent at this stage. But even at this early date, his nudes have greater muscular definition than the blocky emblems that populate Müller's late canvases. And while the brushwork in early Thompson tends to be more blunt and bristly than in subsequent periods, he addresses the canvas in a manner considerably less controlled and less constructive than Müller's.[3]

Ultimately, these distinctions mark the chasm between Thompson's art and abstract expressionist canons. Trained at the Univeristy of Louisville in the late fifties, he was not awed by New York School abstraction, which was widely publicized by then and well-represented in traveling American Federation of Arts shows that came to Louisville's J.B. Speed Museum. Nor did he come to an expressionist mode of figuration exclusively via Tenth Street, although he would have seen "gestural realist"[4] examples by Bob Goodnough, Grace Hartigan and Larry Rivers in shows at the Speed.[5]

76 *Garden of Music*, 1960
oil on canvas
79 x 143 inches
Collection Wadsworth
Atheneum, Hartford; The Ella
Gallup Sumner and Mary
Catlin Sumner Collection

German expressionism was well known and highly influential at Louisville, thanks to several German refugees on the university's art faculty.[6] At the same time, contact with Leon Golub, then teaching at the nearby University of Indiana,[7] ensured knowledge of Chicago's "monster roster" artists, with their combined debt to Dubuffet and to surrealism. Finally, work by Bay Area figure painters David Park and Richard Diebenkorn was displayed in at least two exhibitions that came to Louisville from California museums in 1957 and 1958.[8]

Thus abstract expressionism was but one of several sources of Thompson's expressionist figuration, and in some ways it was the least compelling. The true nature of his artistic concerns would only become apparent during his 1961-63 stay in Europe. There, first in Paris and later in Spain, where the artist and his wife lived on Ibiza before moving to Portintiax, his work gained a new refinement and clarity. His compositions crystallized into vibrant tapestries of flattened forms in bold, unmodulated colors with rhythmically interlocking contours. Now his attachment to Old Master painting was undisguised.

During the 1961-63 period, Thompson frequently lifted whole compositional schemes from such predecessors as Titian, Bosch and Goya. But Thompson rendered Titian's heroes and Goya's goblins in the eye-catching hues and telegraphic language of contemporary comic strips. Although he evidently shared a fondness for vernacular modes with the practitioners of pop art who were emerging in New York at this time, Thompson seems to have preferred updating ancient imagery to elevating modern mass cultural signs.

As if to forestall any confusion of his aims with those of pop art, in his final phase Thompson edged away from the bold simplifications of his previous work. To varying degrees, the late canvases tend toward a greater naturalism, marked by deeper space, more complex design, more detailed drawing and occasional modulation of color. The resulting works, however, remain unmistakable "Bob Thompsons." ■

Judith Wilson

77 *The Assistance of a Woman*, 1960
oil on canvas
61 x 71 inches
Private Collection, courtesy
Vanderwoude Tananbaum
Gallery

Notes

1. Tenor saxophonist Lester Young, known for his porkpie hat.

2. George Nelson Preston (personal communication, December 3, 1987).

3. Müller's influence on Thompson was a posthumous one, primarily transitted by painter Dody Müller after her husband's death.

4. The term is Irving Sandler's. See Sandler, *The New York School: The Painters and Sculptors of the Fifties* (New York: Harper & Row, 1978), esp. pp. 103-121.

5. Hartigan's *Chinatown* and Rivers's *Berdie in the Garden* (1954) both appeared in the Corcoran's *25th Biennial Exhibition—1957*, on view at the J.B. Speed Museum October 2-23, 1957. Goodnough's *Figures* (1956) was included in the *Whitney Annual, 1957*, seen at the Speed February 7-28, 1958.

6. In the years Thompson was a student there, they included the department's head, Dr. Justus Bier, an art historian and former director of the Hanover Kestner Gesellschaft, an important exhibition place for modern German art; the Tobeyesque calligraphic painter Ulfert Wilke, whose personal ties to various German expressionists were a continuation of links formed by his father, a prominent Jugendstil cartoonist; and the painter Carl Crodel.

7. Golub, at the University of Indiana at Bloomington, Wilke, at the University of Louisville, and Frederick Thrusz, at the University of Kentucky at Lexington regularly exchanged visits to one another's classes. Author's interview with Frederick Matys Thursz, New York, October 14, 1986.

8. The exhibitions were Samuel Heavenrich and Grace McCann Morley's *California Painting: 40 Painters*, organized by the Municipal Art Center, Long Beach and the San Francisco Museum of Art, which traveled to the J.B. Speed Museum January 17-February 10, 1957; and the Santa Barbara Museum of Art's *2nd Pacific Coast Biennial Exhibition*, on view at the Speed October 1-22, 1958.

78 *Bird Party*, 1961
oil on canvas
54 x 74 inches
Private Collection, courtesy
Vanderwoude Tananbaum
Gallery

79   *The Journey*, 1962
oil on canvas
80 x 100 inches
Private Collection, courtesy
Vanderwoude Tananbaum
Gallery

80 *The Spinning, Spinning,*
Turning, Directing, 1963
oil on canvas
62⅞ x 82⅞ inches
National Museum of American
Art, Smithsonian Institution,
Gift of Mr. and Mrs. David K.
Anderson, Martha Jackson
Memorial Collection

81 *La Fete*, 1964
oil on canvas
60 x 71 ⅞ inches
Collection Hirshhorn Museum
and Sculpture Garden,
Smithsonian Institution. Gift of
Joseph H. Hirshhorn, 1966

Catalog of the Exhibition

Exhibition Histories 1950-65

Selected Bibliography

Catalog of the Exhibition

Dimensions are in inches, height precedes width. Venues for works not traveling on the entire tour are given in parentheses following their credit lines.

Robert Beauchamp

1 *Tournament of the Witches*, 1959
oil on canvas
60 x 69
Collection The Chrysler Museum, Norfolk, Virginia

2 *Witches*, 1959
oil on canvas
36½ x 46½
Collection Judith and Mitchell Kramer

3 *Untitled*, 1960
oil on canvas
71½ x 90
Archer M. Huntington Art Gallery, University of Texas at Austin; Lent by James and Mari Michener

4 *Untitled*, 1963
oil on canvas
65¾ x 68
Courtesy of the artist

Elaine de Kooning

5 *High Man*, 1954
oil on canvas
79 x 53
Courtesy of the artist

6 *Kaldis in Yellow Chair*, 1954
oil on canvas
63¾ x 49¾
Courtesy of the artist

7 *Harold Rosenberg #III*, 1956
oil on canvas
80 x 59
Courtesy of the artist

8 *Bill at St. Marks*, c. 1956
oil on canvas
72 x 43½
Courtesy of the artist

Willem de Kooning

9 *Untitled Study, Woman (3 Women)*, n.d.
oil on paper
20⅜ x 26⅜
Vassar College Art Gallery, Poughkeepsie, N.Y., Gift of Mrs. Richard Deutsch (Katherine W. Sandford '40), 53.2.5

10 *Two Women on a Wharf*, 1949
oil, enamel, paper and collage on paper
24½ x 24½
Collection Art Gallery of Ontario, Toronto, Canada; Purchase, Membership Endowment Fund, 1977

11 *Warehouse Mannequins*, 1949
oil on board
24 x 34½
Collection Mr. and Mrs. Bagley Wright

12 *Woman*, 1949-50
oil on canvas
64 x 46
Permanent Collection of the Weatherspoon Art Gallery, The University of North Carolina at Greensboro, Lena Kernodle McDuffie Memorial Gift
(PAFA and McNay only)

13 *Reclining Woman*, 1951
pencil on paper
8⅞ x 11¾
Private Collection
(NHAM and PAFA only)

14 *Woman*, 1951
pastel and pencil on paper
11⅞ x 9½
Collection Allan Stone Gallery

15 *Woman*, c. 1951-52
graphite on paper, two-sided drawing
12½ x 9½
Private Collection

16 *Two Women with Still Life*, 1952
pastel on paper
22¼ x 24
Collection Marcia S. Weisman
(NHAM only)

17 *Two Women*, 1952
pencil on paper
12¾ x 12¾
Collection Richard and Mary L. Gray

18 *Woman*, 1952-53
charcoal, crayon and collage on paper
26 x 19
Collection Dr. and Mrs. Martin L. Gecht
(NHAM and PAFA only)

19 *Woman*, c. 1952-53
pastel and pencil on paper
16¾ x 14
Collection Eve Propp
(NHAM and PAFA only)

20 *Woman*, 1953
oil and charcoal on paper mounted on canvas
25⅝ x 19⅝
Hirshhorn Museum and Sculpture Garden, Smithsonian Institution, Gift of Joseph H. Hirshhorn, 1966
(PAFA and McNay only)

21 *Woman I*, 1954
oil on canvas
25¾ x 19½
Sheldon Memorial Art Gallery, University of Nebraska at Lincoln, F.M. Hall Collection

22 *Woman*, 1954
oil on paper
20 x 14⅝
Permanent Collection of the Weatherspoon Art Gallery, The University of North Carolina at Greensboro; Charles and Laura Dwan Memorial Gift

23 *Arrangement in Pink and Green*,
1955
oil on cardboard
21½ x 25½
Seattle Art Museum, Gift of Mrs.
Sidney Gerber and the late Mr. Gerber

24 *Woman*, c. 1955
oil, enamel, charcoal on paper,
mounted on linen
28 x 20
Collection Albright-Knox Art Gallery;
gift of Seymour H. Knox, 1986

25 *Woman*, c. 1955
ink on paper
23½ x 18½
Collection Luke Luyckx

Robert Goodnough

26 *Laocoön I*, 1958
oil on canvas
66⅜ x 54⅛
The Museum of Modern Art, New
York, Given anonymously, 1959

27 *The Bathers*, 1960
oil on canvas
69½ x 74½
Collection Lyda A. Quinn Thomas

28 *Abduction XI*, 1961
oil on canvas
72¼ x 84⅜
National Museum of American Art,
Smithsonian Institution, Gift of S.C.
Johnson & Son, Inc.

29 *Devils in a Boat*, 1963
oil on canvas
84 x 84
Courtesy Vivian Horan Fine Art

Grace Hartigan

30 *The Knight, Death and the Devil
(after Dürer)*, 1952
oil on canvas
66 x 60
Collection Mr. and Mrs. John
T. Ordeman

31 *River Bathers*, 1953
oil on canvas
69⅜ x 88¾
Collection Museum of Modern Art,
New York, Given anonymously, 1954

32 *Grand Street Brides*, 1954
oil on canvas
72 x 102½
Lent by the Whitney Museum of
American Art, New York; Gift of an
anonymous donor, 55.27

33 *The Masker*, 1954
oil on canvas
72 x 41¾
Vassar College Art Gallery, Poughkeepsie, New York, Gallery Purchase, 54.9

34 *Show Case*, 1955
oil on canvas
69¼ x 80¼
The Metropolitan Museum of Art, Roy
R. and Marie S. Neuberger Foundation,
Inc., Fund, 1956 (56.199)

35 *The Vendor*, 1956
oil on canvas
68 x 90
Oklahoma Art Center, Museum
Purchase, Washington Gallery of
Modern Art

Lester Johnson

36 *Three Heads*, 1960
oil on canvas
61¼ x 68½
Collection Lannan Foundation

37 *Broadway Street Scene*, 1962
oil on canvas
60¼ x 78¼
National Museum of American Art,
Smithsonian Institution, Gift of Mr. and
Mrs. David K. Anderson, Martha
Jackson Memorial Collection

38 *Walking Men Green*, 1963
oil on canvas
80¼ x 59⅝
National Museum of American Art,
Smithsonian Institution, Gift of Mr. and
Mrs. David K. Anderson, Martha
Jackson Memorial Collection

39 *Portrait With Feet*, 1963
oil on canvas
80 x 60
Collection of the artist

Alex Katz

40 *Edith and Rudy*, 1957
oil on canvas
36 x 59⅝
Courtesy Robert Miller Gallery

41 *Paul Taylor*, 1959
oil on canvas
66 x 73
Courtesy Robert Miller Gallery

42 *The Black Dress*, 1960
oil on canvas
71½ x 83½
Courtesy Robert Miller Gallery

43 *Rockaway*, 1961
oil on canvas
83 x 72
Courtesy Robert Miller Gallery

George McNeil

44 *Astor*, 1958
oil on canvas
66 x 66
Lent by the Whitney Museum of
American Art, New York; Purchase,
with funds from an anonymous donor.
59.17

45 *Luciana*, 1960
oil on canvas
88 x 80
Collection of the artist, Courtesy M.
Knoedler & Co.

46 *Jezebel*, 1960
oil on canvas
88 x 80
Collection Walker Art Center,
Minneapolis; Gift of the T.B. Walker
Foundation, 1962

47 *Augury*, 1961
oil on canvas
78 x 84
Collection of the artist, Courtesy M.
Knoedler & Co.

Jan Müller

48 *Bacchanale in Sunlight*, 1956
oil on canvas
49⅛ x 96
Solomon R. Guggenheim Museum,
New York, Gift, Mr. and Mrs. Donald
Erenberg, 1985

49 *Of This Time - Of That Place*,
1956
oil on canvas
49½ x 95¾
Collection Mr. and Mrs. John
Martin Shea

50 *Faust I*, 1956
oil on canvas
68⅛ x 120
Collection The Museum of Modern
Art, New York, Purchase, 1957

51 *Walpurgisnacht Faust II*, 1956
oil on canvas
82 x 102½
Collection Howard and Barbara Wise

52 *The Search for the Unicorn*, 1957
oil on canvas
70⅛ x 93⅛
Collection Alfred and Sondra Ordover

53 *The Temptation of St. Anthony*,
1957
oil on canvas
81 x 121½
Lent by the Whitney Museum of
American Art, New York; Purchase.
72.30

54 *The Accusation*, 1957
oil on canvas
48 x 50
Private Collection

55 *Jacob's Ladder*, 1958
oil on canvas
83½ x 115
Solomon R. Guggenheim Museum,
New York

Jackson Pollock

56 *Number 5*, 1952
enamel on canvas
56 x 31½
Collection Modern Art Museum of Fort
Worth, Purchase made possible by a
grant from the Anne Burnett and
Charles Tandy Foundation
(NHAM and PAFA only)

Fairfield Porter

57 *Self-Portrait in the Studio*, c. 1950
oil on canvas
45 x 30
The Parrish Art Museum, Southampton, New York, Gift of the Estate of
Fairfield Porter

58 *Laurance Typing*, 1952
oil on canvas
40 x 30⅛
The Parrish Art Museum, Southampton, New York, Gift of the Estate of
Fairfield Porter

59 *Laurance at the Piano*, 1953
oil on canvas
40 x 30
Courtesy Hirschl & Adler Modern

60 *Katie in an Armchair*, 1954
oil on canvas
65½ x 46
Collection Katherine Porter

61 *Portrait of James Schuyler*, 1955
oil on canvas
48 x 42
Collection Ashby McCulloch
Sutherland

62 *Katie and Anne*, 1955
oil on canvas
80⅛ x 62⅛
Collection Hirshhorn Museum and
Sculpture Garden, Smithsonian
Institution. Gift of Joseph H.
Hirshhorn, 1966

63 *Frank O'Hara*, 1957
oil on canvas
63⅞ x 45⅞
Collection The Toledo Museum of Art;
Gift of Edward Drummond Libbey

64 *Jimmy and John*, 1957-58
oil on canvas
36 x 45½
Collection Barbara K. Goldman,
courtesy Susanne Hilberry Gallery

65 *Anne, Lizzie and Katie*, 1958
oil on canvas
78 x 60
Nebraska Art Association, Thomas C.
Woods Memorial Collection, Courtesy
Sheldon Memorial Art Gallery,
University of Nebraska at Lincoln

66 *Lizzie at the Table*, 1958
oil on canvas
37 x 45
Collection Arthur M. Bullowa
(NHAM only)

Larry Rivers

67 *Two Women Posing*, 1952
oil on canvas
32½ x 53
Collection of the artist

68 *Self-Figure*, 1953
oil and charcoal on canvas
93⅜ x 65½
In the Collection of The Corcoran
Gallery of Art, Museum Purchase,
William A. Clark Fund, 1955
(NHAM and PAFA only)

69 *Berdie in a Red Shawl*, 1953
oil on canvas
53 x 65
Collection Whitney Museum of
American Art; Lawrence H. Bloedel
Bequest 77.1.44

70 *Portrait of Frank O'Hara*, 1954
oil on canvas
97 x 53
Collection of the artist

71 *Double Portrait of Berdie*, 1955
oil on canvas
70¾ x 82½
Collection Whitney Museum of
American Art, New York; Gift of an
anonymous donor, 56.9
(PAFA and McNay only)

72 *The Studio*, 1956
oil on canvas
82½ x 193½
Lent by The Minneapolis Institute of
Arts; The John R. Van Derlip Fund

73 *July*, 1956
oil on canvas
83¼ x 90¼
Collection The Brooklyn Museum,
Anonymous Gift (56.160)

74 *Berdie with the American Flag*,
1957
oil on canvas
20 x 25⅞
The Nelson-Atkins Museum of Art,
Kansas City, Missouri (Gift of
William Inge)

75 *The Last Civil War Veteran*, 1959
oil and charcoal on canvas
82½ x 64⅛
The Museum of Modern Art, New
York, Blanchette Rockefeller Fund,
1962

Bob Thompson

76 *Garden of Music*, 1960
oil on canvas
79 x 143
Collection Wadsworth Atheneum, Hartford; The Ella Gallup Sumner and
Mary Catlin Sumner Collection

77 *The Assistance of a Woman*, 1960
oil on canvas
61 x 71
Private Collection, courtesy Vanderwoude Tananbaum Gallery

78 *Bird Party*, 1961
oil on canvas
54 x 74
Private Collection, courtesy Vanderwoude Tananbaum Gallery

79 *The Journey*, 1962
oil on canvas
80 x 100
Private Collection, courtesy Vanderwoude Tananbaum Gallery

80 *The Spinning, Spinning, Turning,
Directing*, 1963
oil on canvas
62⅞ x 82⅞
National Museum of American Art,
Smithsonian Institution, Gift of Mr. and
Mrs. David K. Anderson, Martha
Jackson Memorial Collection

81 *La Fete*, 1964
oil on canvas
60 x 71⅞
Collection Hirshhorn Museum and
Sculpture Garden, Smithsonian Institution. Gift of Joseph H. Hirshhorn, 1966

Exhibition Histories 1950-65

Robert Beauchamp

Born November 19, 1923 in Denver, Colorado. Studied at Colorado Springs Fine Arts Center, 1942 and 19 46; Cranbrook Art Academy, 1947; Denver University, 1948; and Hans Hofmann School, 1950 to 1953.

Selected Solo Exhibitions

1953 Tanager Gallery, New York; also 1955

1958 March Gallery, New York

1959 Great Jones Gallery, New York; also 1960

1961 Sun Gallery, Provincetown, Massachusetts; also 1963

1963 Green Gallery, New York; also 1964

1964 East End Gallery, Provincetown, Massachusetts; also 1965

Bradford Junior College, Bradford, Massachusetts
HCE Gallery, Provincetown, Massachusetts
Felix Landau Gallery, Los Angeles
Richard Gray Gallery, Chicago

1965 American Gallery, New York

Selected Group Exhibitions

1953 *Rising Talent*, Walker Art Center, Minneapolis

1955 Stable Gallery, New York; also 1956, 1957, 1958
Tanager Gallery, New York; also 1960 and 1961

1956 James Gallery, New York; also 1957

1957 March Gallery, New York; also 1958

1958 *1958 Pittsburgh Bicentennial Exhibition of Contemporary Painting and Sculpture*, Museum of Art, Carnegie Institute, Pittsburgh
Area Gallery, New York
St. Marks in the Bowery, New York

1958 Martha Jackson Gallery, New York
International Arts Gallery, New York
Hansa Gallery, New York

1960 Green Gallery, New York; also 1961
Zabriskie Gallery, New York; also 1961

1961 Visual Arts Gallery, New York
Whitney Museum Biennial, New York; also 1963 and 1965

1962 The Museum of Modern Art, New York
American Gallery, New York
Roland de Aenlle Gallery, New York

Elaine de Kooning

Born March 12, 1920 in New York. Studied at Leonardo da Vinci Art School with Willem de Kooning and Arshile Gorky; Moore College of Art, Philadelphia; and the Western College of Women.

Selected Solo Exhibitions

1952 Stable Gallery, New York; also 1954

1956 Tibor de Nagy Gallery, New York; also 1957

1958 University of New Mexico, Albuquerque

1959 Museum of New Mexico, Santa Fe
Gump's Gallery, San Francisco
Dord Fitz Gallery, Amarillo, Texas; also 1965
Retrospective, Lyman Allyn Museum, New London, Connecticut

1960 Graham Gallery, New York; also 1963 and twice in 1964
Holland Goldowsky Gallery, Chicago
Howard Wise Gallery, Cleveland
Ellison Gallery, Fort Worth, Texas
Roland de Aenlle Gallery, New York

1961 Colby Jr. College, New London, New Hampshire

1962 Louisiana Gallery, Washington, D.C.

1964 Art Gallery Unlimited, San Francisco
University of Nevada, Reno
JFK Portraits, Pennsylvania Academy of Fine Arts, Philadelphia; traveled to Washington Gallery of Modern Art, Washington, D.C.; Harry S. Truman Library, Independence, Missouri; Kansas City Art Institute, Kansas City, Missouri

Selected Group Exhibitions

1951 *9th Street Show*, 60 E. 9th St., New York

1954 *4th International Exhibition*, Tokyo Museum of Art, Tokyo, Japan

1956 *Young American Painters*, The Museum of Modern Art, New York
Expressionism, Walker Art Center, Minneapolis

1957 *Sports in Art*, American Federation of Arts, New York
Lending Library, The Museum of Modern Art, New York
Artists of the New York School: Second Generation, The Jewish Museum, New York

1958 *Action Painting*, Houston Contemporary Art Association, Houston, Texas

1960 *60 American Painters*, Walker Art Center, Minneapolis

1963 *Whitney Annual*, Whitney Museum of American Art, New York

1964 *1964 Pittsburgh International Exhibition of Contemporary Painting and Sculpture*, Museum of Art, Carnegie Institute, Pittsburgh
67th Exhibition, Art Institute of Chicago, Chicago
New Images of Man, The Museum of Modern Art, New York

Willem de Kooning

Born April 24, 1904 in Rotterdam, Holland. Studied at the Academie voor Beeldende Kunsten en Technische Wetenschappen, Rotterdam, 1916-24, and in Brussels and Antwerp, 1924.

Solo Exhibitions

1948 Egan Gallery, New York; also 1951

1953 Sidney Janis Gallery, New York; also 1956, 1959 and 1962
School of the Museum of Fine Arts, Boston

1955 Martha Jackson Gallery, New York

1961 Paul Kantor Gallery, Beverly Hills, California; also 1965

1962 Allan Stone Gallery, New York; also 1964 and 1965

1964 James Goodman Gallery, Buffalo, New York

1965 *Willem de Kooning: A Retrospective Exhibition from Public and Private Collections*, Smith College Museum of Art, Northampton, Massachusetts; traveled to Hayden Gallery and Massachusetts Institute of Technology, Cambridge, Massachusetts

Selected Group Exhibitions

1950 *Annual Exhibition of Contemporary American Painting*, Whitney Museum of American Art, New York; also 1963 and 1965
American Painting, 1950, Virginia Museum, Richmond, Virginia
Confrontations, Sidney Janis Gallery, New York; traveled to the Galerie Nina Causset, Paris, France
American Paintings Annual, California Palace of the Legion of Honor, San Francisco

1951 *Abstract Painting and Sculpture in America*, The Museum of Modern Art, New York
60th Annual, Art Institute of Chicago, Chicago; also 1954

9th Street Show, 60 E. 9th St., New York

1952 *American Vanguard for Paris*, Sidney Janis Gallery, New York; traveled to Galerie de France, Paris, France
Expressionism in American Painting, Albright Art Gallery, Buffalo, New York
1952 Pittsburgh International, Museum of Art, Carnegie Institute, Pittsburgh; also 1955, 1958, 1961 and 1964

1956 *American Artists Paint the City*, 28th Venice Biennale, American Pavilion, Venice, Italy
Recent Paintings by 7 Americans, Sidney Janis Gallery, New York

1957 *8 Americans*, Sidney Janis Gallery, New York; also 1959
Knox Collection, Albright Art Gallery, Buffalo, New York
The '30s Painting in New York, Poindexter Gallery, New York

1958 *Nature in Abstraction*, Whitney Museum of American Art, New York
Fifty Years of Modern Art, Brussels World's Fair, Belgium
New American Painting: As Shown in Eight European Countries 1958-59, The Museum of Modern Art, New York; traveled

1959 *Friends of the Whitney*, Whitney Museum of American Art, New York
Documenta II, Kassel, Germany
New Images of Man, The Museum of Modern Art, New York

1960 *Contemporary American Painting*, Columbus Gallery of Fine Arts, Columbus, Ohio
60 American Painters, 1960, Walker Art Center, Minneapolis
Paths of Abstract Art, Cleveland Museum of Art, Cleveland, Ohio

1961 *The Logic of Modern Art*, William Rockhill Nelson Gallery and Atkins Museum of Fine Arts, Kansas City, Missouri

Ten Americans, Sidney Janis Gallery, New York
American Abstract Expressionists and Imagists, Solomon R. Guggenheim Museum, New York
The Art of Assemblage, The Museum of Modern Art, New York; traveled
Nude in American Painting, The Brooklyn Museum, New York

1962 *Continuity and Change*, Wadsworth Atheneum, Hartford, Connecticut

1963 *Contemporary Painting*, Smith College Museum of Art, Northampton, Massachusetts
Eleven Abstract Expressionist Paintings, Sidney Janis Gallery, New York

1964 *Guggenheim International Award*, Solomon R. Guggenheim Museum, New York
Within the Easel Tradition, Fogg Art Museum, Harvard University, Cambridge, Massachusetts
An Exhibition of American Painting for a Professor of American Art, Smith College Museum of Art, Northampton, Massachusetts
Painting and Sculpture of a Decade: 54/64, Tate Gallery, London, England
Van Gogh and Expressionism in Modern Art, Solomon R. Guggenheim Museum, New York
I. Internationale der Zeichnung, Mathildenhoehe, Darmstadt, Germany

1965 *1943-1953: The Decisive Years*, Institute of Contemporary Art, University of Pennsylvania, Philadelphia
New York School, The First Generation: Paintings of the 1940s and 1950s, Los Angeles County Museum of Art, Los Angeles

Robert Goodnough

Born October 23, 1917 in Cortland, New York. Studied at Syracuse University, B.A. 1940; New York University, M.A.; the New School for Social Research; Ozenfant School of Art; and the Hans Hofmann School of Fine Arts.

Selected Solo Exhibitions

1950 Wittenborn Gallery, New York

1952 Tibor de Nagy Gallery, New York, two exhibitions; also annually through 1970

1956 Museum of Art, Rhode Island School of Design, Providence

1959 Dwan Gallery, Los Angeles; also 1960, 1961 and 1962

1960 Art Institute of Chicago, Chicago; also 1961
Ellison Gallery, Fort Worth, Texas
Jefferson Place Gallery, Washington, D.C.

1961 The Nova Galleries, Boston

1963 James Goodman Gallery, Buffalo, New York

1964 Art Gallery, University of Minnesota, Minneapolis
Art Gallery, University of Notre Dame, South Bend, Indiana
Arts Club of Chicago, Chicago
New Vision Centre Gallery, London, England
U.S. Information Service Gallery, American Embassy, London, England

Selected Group Exhibitions

1950 *New Talent*, Kootz Gallery, New York

1951 Tibor de Nagy Gallery, New York
9th Street Show, 60 E. 9th St., New York

1952 *Paris Vanguard Exhibition*, Paris

1956 *Annual Exhibition of Contemporary American Painting*, Whitney Museum of American Art, New York; also 1957, 1961, 1962, 1963 and 1965

Contemporary New York Painters, Stable Gallery, New York

1957 *American Paintings: 1945-1957*, The Minneapolis Institute of Arts, Minneapolis
The Fourth International Art Exhibition, The Museum of Modern Art, New York
Artists of the New York School: Second Generation, The Jewish Museum, New York

1958 *Nature in Abstraction*, Whitney Museum of American Art, New York
Walter Bareiss Collection, The Museum of Modern Art, New York

1959 *Project I*, Whitney Museum of American Art, New York

1960 *Business Buys American Art*, Whitney Museum of American Art, New York
Sixty American Painters: Abstract Expressionist Painting of the Fifties, Walker Art Center, Minneapolis
The Aldrich Collection, American Federation of Arts, New York; traveled

1961 *Contemporary Paintings from 1960-61 New York Gallery Shows*, Yale University Art Gallery, New Haven, Connecticut
VIIiéme Exposition Internationale de Tunisie, Tunis, Tunisia
Sixty-fourth American Exhibiton, Art Institute of Chicago, Chicago; also 1962
The Art of Assemblage, The Museum of Modern Art, New York Art; traveled to Dallas Museum of Fine Arts and San Francisco Museum of Art, 1962
1961 Pittsburgh International Exhibition of Contemporary Painting and Sculpture, Museum of Art, Carnegie Institute, Pittsburgh
Twenty-seventh Biennial Exhibition of Contemporary Painting, Corcoran Gallery of Art, Washington, D.C.; also 1963

United States Art for Latin America, The Museum of Modern Art, New York

1962 *The S.C. Johnson Collection of Contemporary American Art*, Milwaukee Art Center, Milwaukee; traveled

1963 *Hans Hoffmann and His Students*, The Museum of Modern Art, New York; traveled 1963-1965
International Selection, The Dayton Art Institute, Dayton, Ohio
The Hilton Hotel Collection, The New York Hilton, New York
Two Modern Collectors: Susan Morse Hilles, Richard Brown Baker, Yale University Art Gallery, New Haven, Connecticut

1964 *Annual Exhibition of American Painting and Sculpture*, Pennsylvania Academy of the Fine Arts, Philadelphia
Larry Aldrich Collection, Krannert Art Museum, University of Illinois, Champaign
National Institute of Arts and Letters, New York
New York World's Fair Art Gallery, New York
The Friends Collect, Whitney Museum of American Art, New York

1965 *American Collages*, The Museum of Modern Art, New York
A Decade of Drawings: 1955-1965, Whitney Museum of American Art, New York
Banners, Andre Emmerich Gallery, New York
Northeastern Regional Exhibition of Art Across America, Institute of Contemporary Art, Boston
One Hundred Contemporary American Drawings, Museum of Art, University of Michigan, Ann Arbor

Grace Hartigan

Born March 28, 1922 in Newark, New Jersey. Studied art in Los Angeles, 1941-42, and privately with Isaac Lane Muse in Newark, 1942-47; at Moore College, Philadelphia; Maryland Institute of Art; Coucher College; Towson State University.

Selected Solo Exhibitions

1951 Tibor de Nagy Gallery, New York; also 1952, 1953, 1954, 1955, 1957 and 1959

1955 Vassar College Art Gallery, Poughkeepsie, New York

1959 *Paintings: Summer Work*, Robert Keene Gallery, Southampton, New York

1962 Martha Jackson Gallery, New York; also 1964

Selected Group Exhibitions

1950 *New Talent*, 1950, Kootz Gallery, New York

1951 *9th Street Show*, 60 E. 9th St., New York

1953 *Second Annual Exhibition of Painting and Sculpture*, Stable Gallery, New York; also 1954

1955 *Rising Talent*, Art Gallery, University of Minnesota, Minneapolis

Annual Exhibition of Contemporary American Paintings, Sculpture, Watercolors, Drawings, Whitney Museum of American Art, New York; also 1956, 1957 and 1958

1956 *Twelve Americans* and *Modern Art in the U.S.: Selections from the Collections of The Museum of Modern Art*; traveled in Europe; The Museum of Modern Art, New York

1957 *Third International Art Exhibition*, India
Fourth Annual International Art Exhibition, The Museum of Modern Art, New York; traveled to Japan
Artists of the New York School: Second Generation, The Jewish Museum, New York
IV Bienal, Museum of Modern Art, Sao Paulo, Brazil

1958 *The New American Painting*, organized by The Museum of Modern Art, New York; traveled throughout Europe
New Generation Painters, Art Association of Newport, Cushing Memorial Gallery, Newport, Rhode Island

1959 *New York and Paris: Paintings of the 1950s*, Museum of Fine Arts, Houston, Texas (American section)
Contemporary American Art, World's Fair, Brussels, Belgium

Documenta II, Kassel, Germany
Art U.S.A.: 1959, The Coliseum, New York
School of New York: Some Younger Artists, Stable Gallery, New York

1960 *Contemporary American Painting*, Columbus Gallery of Fine Arts, Columbus, Ohio
Paintings from the Collection of Mr. and Mrs. Patrick B. McGinnis, Chatham College, Pittsburgh
Sixty American Painters, 1960: Abstract Expressionist Painting of the Fifties, Walker Art Center, Minneapolis
Works from Private Collections, Boston University, Boston

1961 *The Face of the Fifties*, Museum of Art, University of Michigan, Ann Arbor
Abstract Expressionists and Imagists, Solomon R. Guggenheim Museum, New York
1961 Pittsburgh International Exhibition of Contemporary Painting and Sculpture, Museum of Art, Carnegie Institute, Pittsburgh
American Vanguard, organized by Solomon R. Guggenheim Museum for the United States Information Agency; traveled to Austria, England, Germany, Yugoslavia.

1964 *A Decade of New Talent*, American Federation of Arts traveling exhibition
Figuration and Defiguration, Museum of Ghent, Belgium

Lester Johnson

Born January 27, 1919 in Minneapolis, Minnesota. Studied at the Minneapolis School of Art, the St. Paul Art School and the Art Institute of Chicago, 1942-47.

Selected Solo Exhibitions

1951 Artists Gallery, New York

1952 Korman Gallery, New York

1955 Zabriskie Gallery, New York; also 1957, 1958, 1959 and 1961

1956 Sun Gallery, Provincetown, Massachusetts; also 1957, 1958, 1959 and 1960

1959 Ellison Gallery, Fort Worth, Texas
City Gallery, New York (two-man exhibition)

1960 HCE Gallery, Provincetown, Massachusetts; also 1962

1961 The Minneapolis Institute of Arts, Minneapolis

Ohio State University Gallery, Columbus

1962 Martha Jackson Gallery, New York; also 1963 and 1964
Holland Gallery, New York
Art Institute of Chicago, Chicago
Dayton Art Institute, Dayton, Ohio
Ohio State University Gallery, Columbus

1965 Donald Morris Gallery, Detroit
Yale University Art Gallery, New

Haven, Connecticut
Anderson-Mayer Gallery, Paris,
France

Selected Group Exhibitions

1951 *Annual Watercolor Exhibition*, Pennsylvania Academy of the Fine Arts,
Philadelphia

1955 *813 Broadway*, 813 Broadway,
New York

1957 *American Painting 1945-57*, The
Minneapolis Institute of Arts,
Minneapolis
*Artists of the New York School:
Second Generation New York*, The
Jewish Museum, New York
Stable Gallery, New York
Pennsylvania Academy of the Fine
Arts, Philadelphia

1958 *Critics Choice*, Baltimore Museum,
Baltimore
Annual, Whitney Museum of
American Art, New York

1959 *100 Works on Paper*, Institute of
Contemporary Art, Boston
Art, U.S.A., Sarah Lawrence Col-
lege, Bronxville, New York
Painting Annual, University of
Colorado, Boulder

Nebraska Art Association, Lincoln
Salzburg Festival, Germany

1960 Felix Landau Gallery, Los Angeles
Figure in Contemporary Painting,
American Federation of Arts,
New York
Critics Choice, City and Town
School, New York
Future Classics, Institute of Contem-
porary Arts, Boston
Graphics 60, American Federation
of Arts, New York
*Pursuit and Measurement of
Excellence*, Weatherspoon Art
Gallery, University of North
Carolina, Greensboro
Nebraska Annual, University of
Nebraska, Lincoln

1961 *Recent Painting and Sculpture*, The
Museum of Modern Art, New York
*1961 Pittsburgh International Exhibi-
tion of Contemporary Painting and
Sculpture*, Museum of Art, Carnegie
Institute, Pittsburgh; also 1964
The Emerging Figure, Contem-
porary Arts Museum, Houston, Texas

1962 *Recent Paintings USA: The Figure*,
The Museum of Modern Art, New York
Recent Trends in Painting, USA, Art
Institute of Chicago, Chicago

1963 *Eleven Americans*, Martha Jackson
Gallery, New York
Show of the Avant-Garde, Lausanne
Museum, Switzerland
Ohio State University Museum,
Columbus
*Selections from the Fort Worth Col-
lections*, Fort Worth Art Center, Fort
Worth, Texas

1964 *The American Conscience*, The
New School for Social Research,
New York
Contemporary American Drawings,
The Solomon R. Guggenheim
Musem, New York
Figuration into Abstraction,
Museum of Ghent, Belgium
*Old One Hundred: Selections from
the Larry Aldrich Contemporary
Collection*, The Larry Aldrich
Museum, Ridgefield, Connecticut

1965 *Selections for Museum Acquisition,
Sale, Group Exhibition*, and *Figura-
tion II*, Martha Jackson Gallery,
New York
American Federation of Arts, New
York; traveled
*The First Bucknell Annual National
Drawing Exhibition*, Bucknell
University, Lewisburg, Pennsylvania

Alex Katz

Born in New York , July 24, 1927. Studied
at the Cooper Union School of Art, New
York, 1946-49 and the Skowhegan School
of Painting and Sculpture, Skowhegan,
Maine, 1949-50.

Selected Solo Exhibitions

1954 Roko Gallery, New York; also 1957

1957 Pennsylvania State University,
University Park

1958 Sun Gallery, Provincetown,
Massachusetts; also 1959

1959 Tanager Gallery, New York; also
1962

1960 Stable Gallery, New York; also 1961

1961 Mili-Jay Gallery, Woodstock,
New York

1963 Thibaut Gallery, New York

1964 Fishbach Gallery, New York; also
two exhibitions in 1965
Grinnel Gallery, Detroit

Selected Group Exhibitions

1953 Tanager Gallery, New York; also
1957

1955 *Stable Annual*, Stable Gallery, New
York; also 1956

1959 *Metropolitan New York Art
Alliance Younger Artists*

1960 Pennsylvania Academy of the Fine
Arts, Philadelphia
David Herbert Gallery, Los Angeles
University of Illinois, Champaign
Virginia Museum, Richmond
Young America 1960, Whitney
Museum of American Art, New
York; traveled

1961 *The Figure: Then and Now*, Visual
Arts Gallery, School of Visual Arts,
New York
Annual, Art Institute of Chicago;
also 1962 and 1964

The Figure, Museum of Fine Arts, Houston, Texas
Colby College, Waterville, Maine

1962 *Shows of Last Year*, Yale University Art Gallery, New Haven, Connecticut
Figure, Kornblee Gallery, New York
Felix Landau Gallery, Los Angeles

1963 *Maine and Its Artists*, Colby College, Waterville, Maine
Rose Art Museum, Brandeis University, Waltham, Massachusetts; traveled

1964 *Contemporary Realism in Figure and Landscape*, Wadsworth Atheneum, Hartford, Connecticut
Two Generations of American Art, Swarthmore College, Swarthmore, Pennsylvania
Colby College, Waterville, Maine
Cross Section of Contemporary Art, American Federation of Arts, New York
Landscapes by Eight Americans, The Museum of Modern Art, New York

1965 *American Figure Painters*, Purdue University, Indianapolis, Indiana
American Collage, The Museum of Modern Art, New York
Figure International, American Federation of Arts, New York

George McNeil

Born February 22, 1908, New York City; studied at Pratt Institute, Art Students League, Hans Hofmann School, Columbia University.

Selected Solo Exhibitions

1950 Egan Gallery, New York; also 1952, 1953 and 1954

1953 Brown Gallery, Boston

1956 M.H. De Young Memorial Museum, San Francisco

1957 Poindexter Gallery, New York; also 1959

1960 Wise Gallery, New York; also 1962 and 1964

1961 Nova Gallery, Boston

Selected Group Exhibitions

1951 *Abstract Art in America*, The Museum of Modern Art, New York
9th Street Show, 60 E. 9th St., New York

1953 Whitney Museum of American Art; also 1957, 1961 and 1965

1961 *Some Contemporary Artists*, Cleveland Museum of Art

American Abstract Expressionists and Imagists, Solomon R. Guggenheim Museum, New York

1962 *66th American Exhibition*, Paris, circulated by the Art Institute of Chicago, 1962-63
Pennsylvania Academy of the Fine Arts

1963 *Directions-Painting USA*, San Francisco Museum of Art

1964 *Recent American Paintings*, Art Galleries, University of Texas at Austin

Jan Müller

Born in Hamburg, Germany, December 27, 1922. Studied at the Art Students League and the Hans Hofmann School of Fine Arts, New York, 1945-50. Died in New York, January 29, 1958.

Selected Solo Exhibitions

1953 Hansa Gallery, New York; also 1954, 1955, 1956, 1958 and 1959

1955 Sun Gallery, Provincetown, Massachusetts; also 1956

1960 Art Gallery, University of Minnesota, Minneapolis

1961 Zabriskie Gallery, New York

1962 Solomon R. Guggenheim Museum, New York (retrospective)

Selected Group Exhibitions

1951 *813 Broadway*, 813 Broadway, New York
Expansionists, House of Duveen, New York

1952 *Group Exhibition of All Members*, Hansa Gallery, New York

1955 *Rising Talent*, University Art Museum, University of Minnesota, Minneapolis

1956 *Stable Show: 1956*, Stable Gallery, New York

12 Painters, Sun Gallery, Provincetown, Massachusetts

1957 *Young America 1957*, Whitney Museum of American Art, New York
Artists of the New York School: Second Generation, The Jewish Museum, New York
6th New York Artists' Annual Exhibition, Stable Gallery, New York
Society for Contemporary American Art, Art Institute of Chicago, Chicago
Fourth International Art Exhibition of Japan, Mainichi Newspapers, Tokyo, and The Museum of Modern Art, New York

Second Generation of the New York School, Felix Landau Gallery, Los Angeles
Painting and Sculpture Acquisitions, The Museum of Modern Art, New York
Annual Exhibition, Whitney Museum of American Art, New York

1958 *New Talent in the USA 1958*, American Federation of Arts, New York; traveled

Festival of Two Worlds, Spoleto, Italy
1958 Pittsburgh Bicentennial International Exhibition of Contemporary Painting and Sculpture, Art Museum, Carnegie Institute, Pittsburgh, Pennsylvania

1959 *100 Works on Paper I, United States*, Institute of Contemporary Art, Boston
New Images of Man, The Museum

of Modern Art, New York
Horace Richter Collection, Mint Museum of Art, Charlotte, North Carolina
The Image Lost and Found, Institute of Contemporary Art, Boston
The Figure in Contemporary American Painting, American Federation of Arts, New York; traveled

Jackson Pollock

Born January 28, 1912 in Cody, Wyoming. Studied with Thomas Hart Benton at the Art Students League, New York, 1926-33. Died August 12, 1956 in East Hampton, Long Island, New York.

Selected Solo Exhibitions

1950 Betty Parsons Gallery, New York; also 1951
Ala Napoleonica (Museo Correr), Piazza di S. Marco, Venice (Peggy Guggenheim collection)

1951 Hilltop Theatre Art Room, Lutherville, Maryland

1952 Sidney Janis Gallery, New York; also 1954, 1955, 1957 and 1958
Studio Paul Fachetti, Paris
A Retrospective Show of the Paintings of Jackson Pollock, Bennington College, Bennington, Vermont

1956 The Museum of Modern Art, New York; also 1967 (traveled to Los Angeles County Museum of Art) and 1968 (traveled extensively)

1957 *IV Bienal*, Museum of Modern Art, Sao Paulo, Brazil

1961 Marlborough Fine Art Ltd., London, England
Kunsthaus, Zurich, Switzerland
Kunstverein für die Rheinlande und Westfalen, Kunsthalle, Düsseldorf, Germany

1962 Toninelli Arte Moderno, Milan, Italy
Marlborough Galleria d'Arte, Rome, Italy

1963 Moderna Museet, Stockholm, Sweden

1964 Marlborough-Gerson Gallery, New York; also 1969
Griffin Gallery, New York

1965 International Council at the The Museum of Modern Art, New York; traveled in Europe

Selected Group Exhibitions

1951 *Ben Shahn, Willem de Kooning, Jackson Pollock*, The Arts Club of Chicago
Surrealisme & Abstractie Keuze uit de Verzameling Peggy Guggenheim, Stedelijk Museum, Amsterdam, Holland
9th Street Show, 60 E. 9th St., New York

1952 *15 Americans*, The Museum of Modern Art, New York

1955 *Tendances Actuelles*, Kunsthalle, Berne, Switzerland

1959 *Documenta II*, Kassel, Germany

1965 *New York School: The First Generation Paintings of the 1940s and 1950s*, Los Angeles County Museum of Art, Los Angeles
The Peggy Guggenheim Collection, Tate Gallery, London, England

Fairfield Porter

Born in Winnetka, Illinois, 1907. B.S. (Fine Arts), Harvard University, 1928. Studied at the Art Students League, New York, in 1930. Died in Southampton, New York, 1975.

Selected Solo Exhibitions

1951 Tibor de Nagy Gallery, New York; also annually to 1971

1959 Art Museum, Rhode Island School of Design, Providence

Larry Rivers

Born August 17, 1923 in New York. Studied at Hans Hofmann School of Fine Arts, New York, 1947-48, and New York University.

Selected Solo Exhibitions

1951 Tibor De Nagy Gallery, New York; also annually from 1952 through 1962, except 1955

1954 Stable Gallery, New York

1961 Martha Jackson Gallery, New York Dwan Gallery, Los Angeles; also 1963

1962 Galerie Rive Droit, Paris, France Gimpel Fils Gallery, London, England; also 1964

1965 *Larry Rivers* (retrospective), Rose Art Museum, Brandeis University, Waltham, Massachusetts; traveled to Pasadena Art Musem, Pasadena, California; The Jewish Museum, New York; Detroit Institute of Arts; The Minneapolis Institute of Arts

Selected Group Exhibitions

1950 *New Talent 1950*, Kootz Gallery, New York

1955 *The 24th Annual Biennial Exhibition of Contemporary Oil Paintings*, Corcoran Gallery of Art, Washington, D.C.; also 1957

1963 University of Alabama, Tuscaloosa University of Illinois, Champaign

1965 Reed College, Portland, Oregon

Selected Group Exhibitions

1951 *9th Street Show*, 60 E. 9th St., New York

1961 *Whitney Annual*, Whitney Museum of American Art, New York; also 1962, 1963, 1964 and 1965 The Museum of Modern Art, New York

1956 *Twelve Americans* and *Recent Drawing U.S.A.*, The Museum of Modern Art, New York

1957 *American Paintings, 1945-1957*, The Minneapolis Institute of Arts, Minneapolis *IV Bienal*, Museum of Modern Art, Sao Paulo, Brazil

1959 *Contemporary American Painting and Sculpture*, Krannert Art Museum, University of Illinois, Champaign; also 1961 *Recent Sculpture U.S.A.*, The Museum of Modern Art, New York

1961 *1961 Pittsburgh International Exhibition of Contemporary Painting and Sculpture*, Museum of Art, Carnegie Institute, Pittsburgh; also 1964 *64th Annual American Exhibition*, Art Institute of Chicago; also 1964 *Disegni Americani Moderni, Festival of Two Worlds*, Spoleto, Italy; assembled and circulated throughout Europe by The Museum of Modern Art, New York

1962 *American Art Since 1950*, Rose Art Museum, Brandeis Universtity, Waltham, Massachusetts *Art U.S.A. Now*, S.C. Johnson Collection, Racine, Wisconsin *Recent Painting U.S.A.*, The Museum of Modern Art, New York *Art Since 1950*, Seattle World's Fair, Seattle, Washington

Yale University Art Gallery, New Haven, Connecticut Dayton Art Institute, Dayton, Ohio

1962 University of Nebraska, Lincoln Kansas City Art Institute, Kansas City, Missouri

1963 Colby College, Waterville, Maine

1964 The Maryland Institute, Baltimore New York World's Fair

1965 University Art Museum, University of New Mexico, Albuquerque

1963 *Brandeis University Recent Acquisitions: The Gevirtz-Munchin Collection and Related Gifts*, Rose Art Museum, Brandeis University, Waltham, Massachusetts; traveled to the Kootz Gallery, New York *Premier Salon International des Galeries Pilotes, Lausanne—Artistes et Decouvreurs de Notre Temps*, Musée Cantonal des Beaux-Arts, Lausanne, Switzerland

1964 *Paintings from The Museum of Modern Art, New York*, National Gallery of Art, Smithsonian Institution, Washington, D.C. *Recent American Drawing*, Rose Art Museum, Brandeis University, Waltham, Massachusetts *The Painter and the Photograph*, University Art Gallery, University of New Mexico, Albuquerque *Painting and Sculpture of a Decade, 1954-1964*, The Tate Gallery, London, England *Documenta II*, Kassel, Germany

1965 *Portraits from the American Art World*, The New School Art Center, New School for Social Research, New York *The New American Realism*, Worcester Art Museum, Worcester, Massachusetts *New Realism*, Gemeentemuseum, The Hague, Holland

Bob Thompson

Born June 26, 1937 in Louisville, Kentucky. Studied at Boston University and the University of Louisville. Died May 30, 1966.

Selected Solo Exhibitions

1960 Delancey Street Museum, New York

1961 Superior Street Gallery, Chicago

1963 Martha Jackson Gallery, New York; also 1965
El Cosorio Gallery, Ibiza, Spain

1964 Paula Johnson Gallery, New York
Richard Gray Gallery, Chicago; also 1965

1965 East End Gallery, Provincetown, Massachusetts
Donald Morris Gallery, Detroit

Selected Group Exhibitions

1958 Provincetown Art Festival, Massachusetts
Arts in Louisville, Louisville, Kentucky

1960 City Gallery, New York
Zabriskie Gallery, New York
American Federation of Arts traveling exhibition (1960-61); also 1962-63 and 1964

1964 The Museum of Modern Art, New York
7 Young Painters, Yale University Art Gallery, New Haven, Connecticut
Farleigh-Dickinson University, Rutherford, New Jersey
International Selection, Dayton Art Institute, Dayton, Ohio

Art Institute of Chicago, Chicago
CORE Exhibition, New York; also 1965
Paula Johnson Gallery, New York
New York: Looking Back, 1964-49, Martha Jackson Gallery, New York; also 1965

1965 *Portraits in the American Art World*, The New School Art Center, The New School for Social Research, New York
Bucknell University, Lewisburg, Pennsylvania
A Survey of Contemporary Art, J.B. Speed Museum, Louisville, Kentucky
Collector's Choice, South Bend Art Center, South Bend, Indiana

Compiled by Peter Kosenko.

Selected Bibliography

General

Books

Ashton, Dore. *The New York School: A Cultural Reckoning*. New York: Viking Press, 1973.

Battcock, Gregory, ed. *The New Art: A Critical Anthology*. New York: Frederick A. Praeger, 1957.

Bronner, Stephen, and Kellner, Douglas, eds. *Passion and Rebellion: The Expressionist Heritage*. New York: Universe Books, 1983.

Calas, Nicolas. *Art in the Age of Risk and Other Essays*. New York: E.P. Dutton, 1968.

Chassman, Neil A., ed. *Poets of the Cities: New York and San Francisco, 1950-1965*. New York: E.P. Dutton, 1974.

Friedman, B.H., ed. *School of New York: Some Younger Artists*. New York: Grove Press, 1959. (Goodnough, Hartigan, Rivers.)

Geldzahler, Henry. *New York Painting and Sculpture: 1940-1970*. New York: E.P. Dutton, 1969.

_____. *American Painting in the Twentieth Century*. New York: The Metropolitan Museum of Art, 1965.

Goodall, Donald Bannard. *Partial Bibliography of American Abstract-Expressionist Painting, 1943-1956*. Austin: University of Texas, 1964.

Greenberg, Clement. *Art and Culture: Critical Essays*. Boston: Beacon Press, 1961.

Hess, Thomas B. *Abstract Painting: Background and American Phase*. New York: Viking Press, 1951.

_____. *The Avant-garde*. New York: Macmillan, 1968.

Hunter, Sam. "U.S.A." In *Art Since 1945*, edited by Will Grohmann, pp. 283-331. New York: Harry N. Abrams, 1958.

_____. *Modern American Painting and Sculpture*. New York: Dell Publishing Company, 1959. (Hartigan).

Janis, Sidney. *Abstract and Surrealist Art in America*. New York: Reynal and Hitchcock, 1944.

Kootz, Samuel M. *New Frontiers in American Painting*. New York: Hastings House, 1943.

Kramer, Hilton. *The Age of the Avant-Garde: An Art Chronicle of 1956-1972*. New York and Evanston, Illinois: Harper and Row, 1962.

Myers, John B. *Tracking the Marvelous*. New York: Random House, 1983.

Motherwell, Robert and Reinhardt, Ad, eds. *Modern Artists in America*. New York: Wittenborn, Schultz, 1952.

O'Hara, Frank. *Art Chronicles: 1954-1966*. New York: George Braziller, 1975.

Richard, Lionel. *The Concise Encyclopedia of Expressionism*. Secaucus, N.J.: Chartwell, 1978.

Rodman, Selden. *Conversations with Artists*. New York: The Devin-Adair Co., 1957.

Rose, Barbara. *American Art Since 1900: A Critical History*. New York: Frederick Praeger, 1967. McNeil.

_____. *American Painting: the 20th Century*. Lausanne, Switzerland: Skira, 1969.

Rosenberg, Harold. *The Tradition of New York*. New York: Horizon Press, 1959.

_____. *The Anxious Object: Art Today and Its Audience*. New York: Horizon Press, 1966.

_____. *Art on the Edge*. New York: Macmillan Publishing, 1975.

Rubinstein, Charlotte. *American Women Artists*. Boston: G.K. Hall & Co., 1982. (E. de Kooning, Hartigan.)

Russell, John. *The Meanings of Modern Art*. Vol. 2: *The Great Divide 1950-70*. New York: Museum of Modern Art, 1975.

Sandler, Irving H. *The New York School: The Painters and Sculptors of the Fifties*. New York: Harper and Row, 1978. (Hartigan.)

_____. *The Triumph of American Painting: A History of Abstract Expressionism*. New York: Harper and Row/Icon Editions, 1970.

Solomon, Alan R. *New York: The New Art Scene*. New York: Holt, Rinehart and Winston, 1967.

Steinberg, Leo. *Other Criteria: Confrontations with 20th-Century Art*. New York: Oxford University Press, 1972.

Exhibition Catalogs

Abstract Expressionist Painting of the Fifties. Minneapolis: Walker Art Center, 1961.

Auping, Michael. *Abstract Expressionism: The Critical Developments*. New York: Harry N. Abrams and Albright-Knox Art Gallery, 1987. (W. de Kooning, Pollock.)

American Abstract Expressionists and Imagists. New York: The Solomon R. Guggenheim Foundation, 1961. (Hartigan.)

Contemporary Art, 1942-72. New York: Praeger Publishers/ Albright-Knox Art Gallery, 1972. Includes Irving Sandler's "Abstract Expressionism."

Expressionism in American Painting. Buffalo: Albright-Knox Gallery, 1952.

Kingsley, April. *Emotional Impact: New York Figurative Expressionism*. San Francisco: The Art Museum Association of America, 1984. (Beauchamp, Hartigan, Johnson, McNeil.)

The New American Painting as Shown in Eight European Countries 1958-1959. New York: The Museum of Modern Art, 1959. (W. de Kooning, Hartigan, Pollock.)

The New York School: Second Generation. New York: The Jewish Museum,

1957. Introduction by Leo Steinberg. (E. de Kooning, Goodnough, Hartigan, Johnson, Müller.)

9th Street Show. Catalog for independent exhibition organized at 60 E. 9th St., New York, 1951. (E. de Kooning, W. de Kooning, Goodnough, Hartigan, McNeil, Pollock, Porter.)

Pressures of the Hand: Expressionist Impulses in Recent American Art. Potsdam, N.Y.: Brainerd Art Gallery, State University of New York, 1984. Curated by Carter Ratcliff.

Rand, Harry. *The Martha Jackson Memorial Collection*. Washington, D.C.: National Museum of American Art, Smithsonian Institution Press, 1985. (Hartigan, Johnson, Katz, Thompson.)

Recent Painting U.S.A.: The Figure. New York: The Museum of Modern Art, 1962.

Rising Talent. Minneapolis: University Gallery, University of Minnesota, 1955. (Hartigan, Müller.)

Rosenzweig, Phyllis. *The Fifties: Aspects of Painting in New York*. Washington, D.C.: Smithsonian Institution Press, 1980.

Schimmel, Paul et al. *Action/Precision: The New Direction in New York, 1955-60*. Newport Beach, California: Newport Harbor Art Museum, 1984. (Hartigan.)

Seckler, Dorothy Gees. *Provincetown Painter 1890s-1970s*. Syracuse, New York: Everson Museum of Art, 1977. (Thompson.)

Sims, Lowery Stokes and Lieverman, William S. *The Figure in 20th Century American Art: Selections from the Metropolitan Museum of Art*. New York: The American Federation of Arts and the Metropolitan Museum of Art, 1984. (Thompson.)

60 American Painters: Abstract Expressionist Painting of the Fifties. Nancy Miller, ed. Minneapolis: Walker Art Center, 1961. (E. de Kooning, Hartigan.)

Selz, Peter. *New Images of Man*. New York: Museum of Modern Art, 1961. Statements by the artists. (W. de Kooning, Müller, Pollock.)

Styron, Thomas W. *American Figurative Painting 1950-1980*. Norfolk, Virginia: The Chrysler Museum, 1980. (Thompson.)

12 Americans. Dorothy Miller, ed. New York: Museum of Modern Art, 1956.

Tuchman, Maurice. *New York School: The First Generation: Painting of the 1940s and 1950s*. Los Angeles: Los Angeles County Museum of Art, 1965.

Periodicals

Alloway, Lawrence. "Art In New York Today." *The Listener* (BBC journal) (23 Oct. 1958).

_____ . "Background to Action." *Art News and Review* (18 January 1954), pp. 3-4.

_____ . "Before and After 1945: Reflections on Documenta II." *Art International* 3, no. 7 (1959), pp. 29-36.

_____ . "Gesture into Form." *Art News* 71 (April 1972), pp. 42-44.

"The New American Painting." *Art International* 3, nos. 3-4 (1959).

Armstrong, Richard. "Abstract Expressionism was an American Revolution." *Canadian Art* 21 (September/October 1964), pp. 262-65.

Arnason, H.H. "New Talent in the U.S." *Art in America* 46 (Spring 1958), p. 16.

Ashton, Dore. "La Signature Americaine." *XXe Siécle* (March 1958).

_____ . "Museum of Modern Art's Sixteen Americans Exhibition." *Arts and Architecture* (February 1960), p. 2.

_____ . "Some Lyricists in the New York School." *Art News and Review* (22 November 1958), pp. 3, 8.

Battcock, Gregory. "It is." *Arts Magazine* 48 (April 1974), pp. 31-33.

Brach, Paul. "Postscript: The Fifties." *Artforum* (September 1965), p. 32.

Butler, Barbara. "New York Fall 1961." *Quadrum* no. 12 (1962), pp. 133-40, 185.

Campbell, Lawrence. "New Figures at Uptown Whitney." *Art News* 53 (February 1955), pp. 34-35.

_____ . "American Figurative Expressionism." *Art in America* 81 (December 1982).

Donnel, Radka. "Space in Abstract Expressionism." *Journal of Aesthetics and Art Criticism* 23 (Winter 1964), pp. 239-49.

"Documenta II, Kassel, Art After 1945." *Cimaise* (September/November 1959), pp. 38-57.

"813 Broadway." *Arts Digest* 26 (15 December 1951), p. 17.

"The Expansionists." *Arts Digest* 26 (1 January 1952), pp. 20-21.

Farber, Manny. "New Images of (ugh) Man." *Art News* 58 (October 1959), p. 58.

Ferren, John. "Epitaph for an Avant-Garde: The Motivating Ideas of the Abstract Expressionist Movement as Seen by an Artist Active on the New York Scene." *Arts Magazine* 33 (November 1958), pp. 24-26, 68.

Finkelstein, Louis. "New Look: Abstract-Expressionism." *Art News* 55 (March 1956), pp. 36-39, 66-68.

Frumkin, Allan. "The Figurative Tradition." *Arts Magazine* 55 (September 1980), p. 9.

Fussiner, Howard. "The Use of Subject Matter in Recent Art." *The Art Journal* 20 (Spring 1961), pp. 134, 137.

Genauer, Emily. "'Sensational' Show at the Jewish Museum." *New York Herald Tribune* (29 September 1965), p. 17.

Golub, Leon. "A Critique of Abstract Expressionism." *College Art Journal* 14 (Winter 1955).

Goldwater, Robert. "Everyone Knew What Everyone Else Meant." *It is* (Autumn 1959), p. 4.

_____ . "Reflections on the New York School." *Quadrum* no. 8 (1960), pp. 17-36.

Goossen, Eugene. "The Big Canvas." *Art International* 2, no. 8 (1958).

Greenberg, Clement. "Abstract and Representational." *Arts Digest* 29 (1 November 1954), pp. 6-8.

_____ . "The Crisis of Abstract Art." *Arts Yearbook* 7 (1964), pp. 89-92.

_____ . "New York Painting Only Yesterday." *Art News* 56 (Summer 1957), pp. 58-59, 84-86.

_____ . "After Abstract Expressionism." *Art International* 6 (October 1962), pp. 24-32.

Hess, Thomas B. "Introduction to Abstract." *Art News Annual* 20 (1950), pp. 127-58.

_____ . "The Many Deaths of American Art." *Art News* 59 (October 1960), p. 25.

_____ . "Mixed Pickings from the Fat Years." *Art News* 54 (Summer 1955), p. 78.

_____ . "Seeing the Young New Yorkers." *Art News* 50 (November 1952), pp. 23, 60.

_____ . "U.S. Painting: Some Recent Directions." *Art News Annual* 25 (1956), p. 88.

Hunter, Sam. "Abstract Expressionism Then and Now." *Canadian Art* 21 (September 1964), p. 267.

"Is There a New Academy?" Parts I and II. *Art News* 58 (Summer 1959), pp. 34-37, 58-59; and (September 1959), pp. 36-39, 58-60.

Kozloff, Max. "American Painting During the Cold War." *Artforum* (May 1973), pp. 32-35.

_____ . "The Dilemma of Expressionism." *Artforum* 3 (November 1964), pp. 32-35.

Kramer, Hilton. "Report on the Carnegie International." *Arts Magazine* 33 (January 1959), pp. 30-37.

_____ . "The New American Painting." *Partisan Review* 20 (July/August 1953), pp. 421-27.

_____ . "Twenty Five Years of the Moderns." *Arts Digest* 29 (1 November 1954), pp. 14-16.

Kunstwerk 15 (November 1961), p. 60. Review of *American Abstract Expressionists and Imagists* at the Guggenheim.

Kuspit, Donald. "Individual and Mass Identity in Urban Art: The New York Case." *Art in America* 65 (September/October 1977), pp. 66-77.

Laderman, Gabriel. "Figurative Painting of the Fifties." *Artforum* 6 (January 1968), pp. 38-57.

Leider, Philip. "New York School: The First Generation." *Artforum* 4 (September 1965), pp. 3-13.

McBride, Henry. "Abstract Report for April: Exhibition at the Sidney Janis Gallery." *Art News* 52 (April 1953), pp. 16-19, 47.

McMullen, Roy. "L'Ecole de New York: des concurrents dangereux." *Connaissance des arts* (September 1961), pp. 30-37.

Munro, Eleanor. "The Found Generation." *Art News* 60 (November 1961), p. 39.

Newgass, F. "New Records for Abstract Art." *Arts Magazine* 39 (February 1965), p. 22.

"New Images of Man." *The Studio* no. 159 (February 1960), p. 53.

"New York School on the Block." *Art in America* 52 (April 1964), p. 105.

O'Hara, Frank. "Panel: All-Over Painting." *It is* (Autumn 1958), pp. 72-78.

Pearlstein, Philip. "Figure Paintings Today are not Made in Heaven." *Art News* 61 (Summer 1962), p 52.

Peterson, Valerie. "U.S. Figure Painting: Continuity and Cliché." *Art News* 61 (Summer 1962), p. 52.

"The Present Outlook on Figurative Painting." *Arts Yearbook* 5 (1961), p. 38.

Preston, Stuart. "Diverse Exhibitions: Expressionist." *New York Times* (7 October 1952), p. 9.

Ratcliff, Carter. "Expressionism Today: An Artist's Symposium." *Art in America* (December 1982), p. 70.

_____ . "The Short Life of the Sincere Stroke." *Art in America* 71 (January 1983), pp. 73-79, 137.

Raynor, Vivien. "Creative Process at the New York School." *Arts Magazine* 35 (September 1961), p. 38.

Read, Sir Herbert and Arnason, H.H. "Dialogue on Modern U.S. Painting: Sir Herbert Read and H.H. Arnason Discuss American Abstract Expressionist Art Currently on View at Walker Art Center." *Art News* 59 (May 1960), pp. 32-36.

"The Reappearing Figure." *Time* (25 May 1962), p. 62.

Remenick, Seymour. "Master Teacher [Hans Hofmann]." *Life* (8 April 1957), p. 70.

Rose, Barbara. "The Second Generation: Academy and Breakthrough." *Artforum* 4 (September 1965), pp. 53-63.

Rosenblum, Robert. "Abstract Sublime." *Art News* 59 (February 1961), pp. 38-41.

Rosenberg, Harold. "The American Action Painters." *Art News* 51 (December 1952), pp. 22-23.

Rubin, William. "The New York School—Then and Now." Parts I and II. *Art International* (March/April 1958), pp. 23-26; (May/June 1958), pp. 19-22.

_____. "Letters from New York." *Art International* (January/March 1959), pp. 6-35.

_____. "Younger American Painters." *Art International* 6, no. 1 (1960), pp. 24-31.

Sandler, Irving H. "New Cool Art." *Art in America* 53 (February 1965), p. 99.

Schapiro, Meyer. "The Younger American Painters of Today." *The Listener* (BBC journal) (26 January 1956), pp. 146-47.

Selz, Peter. "Nouvelles Images de l'homme." *L'Oeil* (February 1960), pp. 46-53.

Siegel, Jeanne. "Abstraction and Representation Made Visible." *Arts Magazine* 51 (November 1976), pp. 70-73.

Smith, Roberta. "Report from Washington: The '50s Revisited, Not Revised." *Art in America* 68 (November 1980), pp. 47-51.

Steinberg, Leo. "Month in Review." *Arts Magazine* 30 (January 1956), p. 78.

Tillim, Sidney. "The Figure and the Figurative in Abstract Expressionism." *Artforum* 4 (September 1965), pp. 45-48.

_____. "Guggenheim Museum's Abstract Expressionists and Imagists." *Arts Magazine* 36 (December 1961), pp. 42-43.

Tyler, Parker. "Is Today's Artist With or Against the Past?" Parts I and II. *Art News* 57 (Summer 1958), pp. 26-29, 42-45, 54-58; and (September 1958), pp. 38-41, 58-63. Interviews with W. de Kooning, Goodnough and Hartigan.

"The Wild Ones." *Time* (20 February 1956).

Robert Beauchamp

Books and Exhibition Catalogs

Robert Beauchamp. Tampa: Florida Center for the Arts, University of South Florida, 1974.

Kuchta, Ronald A., ed. *Robert Beauchamp: An American Expressionist*. Syracuse, N.Y.: Everson Museum of Art, 1984. Essay by April Kingsley and self-interview by the artist.

Oscarsson, Victoria. *Language of Symbols*. New York: Landmark Gallery, 1980.

Sanguinetti, E.F. and Burton, Scott.

Periodicals

Ashton, Dore. "Art U.S.A., 1962." *Studio International* no. 163 (March 1962), p. 91.

_____. *Arts and Architecture* 79 (February 1962), p. 7. Exhibition at Green Gallery.

_____. "On the Way to the Fair. New York Commentary." *Studio International* (September 1964).

Brown, Rosalind. "Reviews and Previews." *Art News* 63 (February 1965), p. 15.

Burnside, Madeleine. "Robert Beauchamp." *Arts Magazine* 54 (February 1980), p. 42.

Burton, Scott. "Paint the Devil." *Art News* 65 (April 1966).

Canaday, John. "Paintings by Robert Beauchamp." *Arts Magazine* 54 (February 1980), p. 42.

Edgar, Natalie. "Reviews and Previews." *Art News* 59 (October 1961).

_____. "Reviews and Previews: Three Live-Wire Painters." *Art News* 61 (February 1963), p. 15.

Faunce, Sarah C. "Reviews and Previews." *Art News* 62 (December 1963), p. 54.

Goldin, Amy. "In the Galleries." *Arts Magazine* 40 (June 1966), p. 49.

Hale, Nike. "Beauchamp's Paintings – Bold Anatomy of Grief." *Art World* (16 October 1978), pp. 1, 8.

Kingsley, April. "Reviews and Previews." *Art News* 71 (March 1972), p. 10.

_____. "Abstract Ex: When in the Course of Human Events . . ." *The Village Voice* (23 October 1978), pp. 113-14.

_____. "Peaceful Contemplation, Violence, and Grandeur." *Soho Weekly News* (20 May 1976), pp. 19-20.

Kramer, Hilton. "Recent Paintings by Robert Beauchamp." *New York Times* (21 May 1976), Section 3, p. 16.

Marter, Joan. "Robert Beauchamp: Haunting Images." *Arts Magazine* 53 (February 1979), pp. 146-47.

Pearlstein, Philip, et. al. "All Beauchamp!!" *Scrap* (9 December, 1960), p. 3.

_____. "Review of Exhibitions: Robert Beauchamp at Monique Knowlton." *Art in America* (March/April 1979), p. 151.

Raynor, Vivien. *Arts Magazine* 38 (January 1964), p. 31. Exhibition at Green Gallery.

Schwartz, Ellen. "Birth of Abstract Expressionism." *Art News* 78 (January 1979), pp. 75-76.

Sedgewick, John. "Robert Beauchamp on Painting." *Apelles: The Georgia Arts Journal 2 (1982), no 2, pp. 2-9.

Tillim, Sidney. Arts Magazine* 36 (October 1961), p. 14. Exhibition at Green Gallery.

Unattributed/Untitled Reviews

Art News 54 (May 1955), p. 54. Exhibition at Tanager Gallery.

Art News 55 (May 1956), p. 50. Exhibition at Hansa Gallery.

Art News 58 (October 1959), p. 58. Exhibition at Great Jones Gallery.

Art News 59 (December 1960), p. 18. Exhibition at Great Jones Gallery.

Art News 60 (October 1961), p. 11. Exhibition at Green Gallery.

Art News 63 (February 1965), p. 15. Exhibition at American Gallery.

Arts Digest 29 (15 April 1955), p. 30. Exhibition of Paintings at Tanager Gallery.

Arts Magazine 30 (May 1956), p. 51. Exhibition at Hansa Gallery.

Elaine de Kooning

Books and Exhibition Catalogs

Bujeses, A., ed. *Twenty-Five Artists*. University Publications of America, 1982.

Fine, E.H. *Women in Art*. Montclair, New Jersey: 1978.

Hess, Thomas B. and Rosenberg, Harold. *Action Painting . . . 1958*. Dallas: Dallas Museum of Contemporary Arts, 1958.

Matsumoto, M. *Portraits of New York Women*. Tohjusha, Japan: 1983.

Munro, E. *Originals: American Women Artists*. New York: 1979.

Periodicals

Bouche, R. "Portrait." *Art in America* 46 (Winter 1958/59), p. 26.

Brumer, Miriam, "New York Reviews." *Art News* 85 (October 1986), pp. 135-36.

Butler, H.C. "Elaine de Kooning." *Horizon* (June 1981).

Campbell, Lawrence. "Elaine de Kooning: Portraits in a New York Scene." *Art News* 62 (April 1963).

_____ . "Elaine de Kooning Paints a Picture." *Art News* 59 (December 1960), pp. 40-43.

_____ . *Art News* 59 (December 1960) pp. 3, 13. Exhibition at Graham Gallery.

_____ . "New Blood in the Old Cross-Section." *Art News* 60 (January 1962), p. 39.

_____ . "Elaine de Kooning at Gruenebaum." *Art in America* (January 1983), p 119.

Crehan, Hubert. *Art News* 58 (February 1960), p. 14. Exhibiton at Tanager Gallery.

De Kooning, Elaine. "Discussion: Is There a New Academy?" *Art News* 58 (June 1959), p. 19.

_____ . "Hans Hoffman Paints a Picture." *Art News* 48 (February 1950), pp. 38-41.

_____ . "Painting a Portrait of the President." *Art News* 63 (Summer 1964), p. 37.

_____ . "Prejudices, Preferences, and Preoccupations." *It is* (Spring 1958) p. 19.

_____ . "Statement." *It is* (Autumn 1959), p. 29.

_____ . "Subject: What, How or Who?" *Art News* 54 (April 1955) pp. 26-29.

"First One-Man Show of Paintings and Drawings at Stable Gallery." *Arts Digest* 28 (15 April 1954), p. 23.

Gray, C. and Lipman, J. "The Amazing Inventiveness of Women Painters." *Cosmopolitan* (October 1961).

Harrison, Helen A. "Elaine de Kooning's Vibrant Portraits." *New York Times* (24 October 1982).

Henry, G. "Artists and the Face: A Modern American Sampling." *Art in America* 42 (April 1954).

_____ . "Elaine de Kooning and Alice Neel." *Art News* 83 (March 1984), p. 210.

Mellow, James R. "In The Galleries." *Arts Magazine* 30 (June 1956). Exhibition at Stable Gallery.

North, C. "Elaine de Kooning at Graham." *Art in America* 64 (May 1976), pp 108-09.

Porter, Fairfield. "Exhibition, Work of the Last Five Years at Stable Gallery." *Art News* 53 (April 1954), p. 45.

"Quest for a Famous Likeness." *Life* (8 May 1964).

Sawin, Martica. "Reviews and Previews." *Arts Magazine* 32 (December 1957), p. 55. Exhibition at De Nagy Gallery.

Schaenfeld, Ann. "Elaine de Kooning." *Arts Magazine* 57 (December 1982), p. 41.

Schuyler, James. "Reviews and Previews." *Art News* 56 (November 1957), p. 12. Exhibition at De Nagy Gallery.

_____ . "Elaine de Kooning." *Art News* 56 (November 1957), p. 12.

Tyler, Parker. *Art News* 55 (May 1956), p. 51. Exhibition at Stable Gallery.

Willem de Kooning

Books and Exhibition Catalogs

Ashton, Dore. *Willem de Kooning: A Retrospective Exhibition from Public and Private Collections*. Massachusetts: Smith College Museum of Art, 1965. Statement by Willem de Kooning.

Blesh, Rudi and Janis, Harriet. *De Kooning*. Evergreen Gallery Book no. 8. New York: Grove Press, 1960.

Cummings, Paul, et al. *Willem de Kooning: Drawings, Paintings, Sculpture*. New York, Munich and London: Whitney Museum of American Art, Prestel-Verlag, and W.W. Norton & Co., 1983.

De Kooning/Cornell. New York: Allan Stone Gallery, 1964.

De Kooning's Women. New York: Allan Stone Gallery, 1966.

Gaugh, Harry F. *Willem de Kooning*. New York: Abbeville, 1983. (Modern Masters Series.)

Goodman, Merle. *"Woman" Drawings by Willem de Kooning*. Buffalo, New York: James Goodman Gallery, 1964.

Greenberg, Clement. Catalogue of de Kooning Retrospective. Boston: School of the Museum of Fine Arts, 1953.

Hess, Thomas B. *Willem de Kooning*. The Great American Artist Series. New York: George Braziller, 1959.

Recent Oils by Willem de Kooning. Foreword by K. Sawyer. New York: Martha Jackson Gallery, 1955.

Recent Paintings by Willem de Kooning. Introduction by Thomas B. Hess. New York: Sidney Janis Gallery, 1962.

Rosenberg, Harold. *Willem de Kooning*. Statements by and interview with de Kooning. New York: Harry N. Abrams, 1974.

Willem de Kooning. Essay by Clifford Odets. Beverly Hills, California: Paul Kantor Gallery, 1961.

Willem de Kooning. Pittsburgh: Museum of Art, Carnegie Institute, 1980. With selections from the writings of Willem de Kooning.

Willem de Kooning. Preface by William Inge. Beverly Hills, California: Paul Kantor Gallery, 1965.

Wolfe, Judith. *Willem de Kooning: Works from 1951-1981*. Photographs of de Kooning by Hans Namuth. East Hampton, New York: Guild Hall, 1981.

Yard, Sally E. *Willem de Kooning: The First Twenty-six Years in New York, 1927-1952*. Ph.D. dissertation, Princeton University, 1980.

Periodicals

Alloway, Lawrence. "Sign and Surface: Notes on Black and White Painting in New York." *Quadrum* no. 9 (1960), p. 51.

_____ . "De Kooning: Criticism and Art History." *Artforum* 13 (January 1975), pp. 46-50.

Ashton, Dore. "Art." *Arts and Architecture* 76 (March 1959), p. 8.

_____ . "Art: Willem de Kooning." *Arts and Architecture* 76 (July 1959), pp. 5, 30-31.

_____ . "Art: Sidney Janis' Recent Exhibition of Eight Painters." *Arts and Architecture* 74 (June 1957), p. 9.

_____ . "Exhibition of Twenty-one Works by de Kooning at the Martha Jackson Gallery." *Arts and Architecture* 72 (December 1955), pp. 33-34.

_____ . "New York Commentary: de Kooning's Verve." *Studio International* no. 163 (June 1962), pp. 216-17, 224.

Bannard, Walter Darby. "Willem de Kooning's Retrospective at the Museum of Modern Art." *Artforum* 7 (April 1969), pp. 42-49.

Barr, Alfred H., Jr. "Seven Americans Open in Venice." *Art News* 49 (June 1950), pp. 22-23.

Battcock, Gregory. "Big Splash." *Time* (18 May 1959), p. 72.

_____ . "Willem de Kooning." *Arts Magazine* 42 (November 1967), pp. 34-37.

"Big City Dames." *Time* (6 April 1953), p. 80.

Calas, Nicolas. "Venus: de Kooning and the Woman." *Arts Magazine* 43 (April 1969), p. 22.

Coates, Robert M. "Art Galleries: Exhibition of New Paintings by Willem de Kooning." *The New Yorker* (4 April 1953), p. 96.

Crehan, Hubert. "Woman Trouble." *Arts Digest* 27 (15 April 1953), pp. 4-5.

"De Kooning's Masterwork: Women of 1950-55." *Time* (7 March 1969), p. 61.

Faison, S. Lane, Jr. "Art: Exhibition at the Sidney Janis Gallery." *The Nation* (18 April 1953), pp. 333-34.

Farber, Manny. "Art: Group Exhibition at the Sidney Janis Gallery." *The Nation* (11 November 1950), pp. 445-46.

Finkelstein, Louis. "Marin and de Kooning." *Magazine of Art* 43 (October 1950), pp. 202-6.

_____ . "Light of de Kooning." *Art News* 66 (November 1967), pp. 28-31.

Fitzsimmons, James. "Art: Exhibition at Sidney Janis Gallery." *Arts and Architecture* 70 (May 1953), pp. 4, 6-8.

Forge, Andrew. "De Kooning's 'Women' at the Tate Gallery." *Studio International* no. 176 (December 1968), pp. 246-51.

Frankenstein, Alfred. "The de Kooning Figure Merely Went Underground." *San Francisco Chronicle* (16 March 1969), This World Magazine, pp. 41-43.

Geist, Sidney. "New York: De Kooning Studies and Paintings at the Janis Gallery." *Arts Digest* 26 (1 April 1952), p. 15.

Genauer, Emily. "De Kooning a Puzzle." *New York World-Telegram* (4 May 1948).

Glueck, Grace. "The Twentieth Century Artists Most Admired by Other Artists." *Art News* 76 (November 1977), pp. 78-103.

Hammacher, A.M. "Mondrian and de Kooning: A Contrast in Transformation." *Delta* 2 (September 1959), pp. 67-71.

Henning, E.B. "Language of Art." *Cleveland Museum of Art Bulletin 51* (November 1964), p. 216.

Hess, Thomas B. "De Kooning Paints a Picture." *Art News* 52 (March 1953), pp. 30-33.

_____ . "De Kooning's New Women." *Art News* 64 (March 1965), pp. 36-38.

_____ . "Is Today's Artist With or Against the Past?" *Art News* 57 (Summer 1958), pp. 27, 56. Interview.

O'Doherty, Brian. "De Kooning: Grand Style." *Newsweek* (4 January 1965), pp. 56-57. Reprinted in Brian O'Doherty, *Object and Idea: An Art Critic's Journal, 1961-67*. New York: Simon & Schuster, 1967.

_____ . Willem de Kooning: Fragmentary Notes Toward a Figure." *Art International* 12 (Christmas 1968), pp. 21-29. Reprinted in Brian O'Doherty, *American Masters: The Voice and the Myth*. New York: Random House, 1974.

Porter, Fairfield. "Reviews and Previews: Willem de Kooning." *Art News* 54 (November 1955), pp. 48-49.

Raynor, Vivien. "Art: An Anthology of American Nudes." *New York Times* (24 February 1978), Section 3, p. 19.

Rosenblum, Robert. "Gorky, Matta, de Kooning, Pollock at the Janis Gallery." *Arts Digest* 29 (1 June 1955), p. 24.

Russell, John. "Art: Drawing Reborn in de Kooning's Painted Women." *New York Times* (14 September 1974), p. L24.

Sawyer, Kenneth B. "Backyard on Tenth Street." *Baltimore Museum of Art News* 20 (December 1956), pp. 3-7.

_____ . "Three Phases of Willem de Kooning." *Art News and Review* 22 (22 November 1958), pp. 4-16.

"Spotlight on de Kooning." *Art News* 47 (April 1948), p. 33.

Steinberg, Leo. "De Kooning Shows Recent Painting in 'Woman' Series at Jackson Gallery." *Arts Magazine* 30 (March 1955), pp. 46-47. Reprinted in Leo Steinberg, *Other Criteria: Confrontations with Twentieth-Century Art*. London, Oxford and New York: Oxford University Press, 1972.

Tillim, Sidney. "Willem de Kooning." *Arts Magazine* 33 (June 1959), pp. 54-55.

"What Abstract Art Means to Me." *The Museum of Modern Art Bulletin* (Spring 1951), pp. 1-15. Symposium at The Museum of Modern Art including Willem de Kooning.

Yard, Sally E. "De Kooning's Women." *Arts Magazine* 53 (November 1978), pp. 96-101.

Zimmer, William. "De Kooning at the Guggenheim: Women as Source." *Soho Weekly News* (23 February 1978), p. 20.

Robert Goodnough

Books and Exhibition Catalogs

Bush, Martin H. *Goodnough*. New York: Abbeville Press, 1982. Foreword by Clement Greenberg.

Bush, Martin H., and Moffett, Kenworth. *Goodnough*. Wichita, Kansas: Ulrich Museum of Art, Wichita State University, 1973.

Friedman, B.H. *Goodnough*. Los Angeles, California: Dwan Gallery, 1960.

Goodnough, Major Works: 1957-1968. New York: Tibor de Nagy Gallery, 1985.

Guest, Barbara, and Friedman, B.H. *Goodnough*. Paris: Editions Georges Fall, 1962.

Lauck, Anthony. *Looking Backward from Robert Goodnough*. South Bend, Indiana: University of Notre Dame, 1967.

Love, Richard. *Goodnough*. Chicago: Haase-Mumm Publishing Co., 1987.

Robert Goodnough: Cubism in Transition. New York, Shippee Gallery, 1988. Foreword by André Emmerich.

Robert Goodnough. Syracuse, New York: Syracuse University Lubin House Gallery, 1972.

Periodicals

Arts Digest 25 (15 October 1950), p. 20. Exhibition at Wittenborn Gallery.

Ashton, Dore. "Art." *Arts and Architecture* (March 1960), p. 35.

_____ . "Art." *Arts and Architecture* (May 1962), p. 7.

_____ . "Art: Paintings by Robert Goodnough." *New York Times* (6 January 1959).

_____ . "Recent Exhibition at Tibor de Nagy Gallery." *Arts and Architecture* (March 1961), p. 6.

_____ . "Robert Goodnough." *Arts Digest* (15 November 1952), p. 23.

_____ . "Robert Goodnough." *Studio International* (1 July 1962), p. 8.

Benedikt, Michael. "Robert Goodnough." *Art News* 64 (March 1965), p. 12.

Brach, Paul. "Robert Goodnough." *Arts Digest* (1 February 1952), p. 18.

Butler, Barbara. "Brach, Goldberg, Goodnough, Mitchell." *Arts Magazine* 30 (June 1956), pp. 48-49.

Campbell, Lawrence. "Robert Good-nough." *Art News* 54 (May 1955), p. 48.

Faulkner, Joseph W. "Goodnough's Spirited Art Stirs Up Thoughts of the New York School." *Chicago Tribune* (15 March 1964).

Forge, Andrew. "Know-how." *New Statesman* (28 August 1964), p. 294.

Goodnough, Robert. "About Painting." *Art and Literature: An International Review* (Autumn 1965), pp. 119-127.

_____ . "Franz Kline Paints a Picture." *Art News* 51 (December 1952), pp. 36-39.

_____ . "Jackson Pollock Paints a Picture." *Art News* 50 (May 1951), pp. 38-41.

Gray, Leve. "New Venture—The Hilton Hotel Collection" *Art in America* (April 1963), p. 124.

Hughes, Robert. "Abstract Energy." *Observer* (London) (23 August 1964).

Judd, Donald. "Robert Goodnough." *Arts Magazine* 35 (February 1961), p. 53.

_____ . "Robert Goodnough." *Arts Magazine* 36 (May 1962), p. 98.

Kind, Joshua. *Art News* 63 (May 1964), pp. 21-22. Exhibition at Arts Club, Chicago.

LaFarge, Henry A. "Robert Goodnough." *Art News* 49 (November 1950), p. 47.

Langsner, Jules. *Art News* 59 (Summer 1960), p. 56. Exhibition at Dwan Gallery, Los Angeles.

Mayer, Ralph. "Robert Goodnough" *Arts Digest* (15 March 1954).

Munro, Eleanor C. *Art News* 55 (June 1956), p. 50. Exhibition *Four Americans* at Janis Gallery, New York.

Munsterberg, Hugo. "Robert Goodnough." *Arts Magazine* 34 (January 1960), p. 49.

O'Doherty, Brian. "Oh! Say Can You See." *Newsweek* (11 January 1965), p. 78.

O'Hara, Frank. "Goodnough gazed on Euclid Bare: New Paintings at De Nagy." *Art News* 53 (March 1954), p. 18.

Pease, Roland F., Jr. "Robert Goodnough." *Metro* 9 (April 1962), pp. 57-61.

Porter, Fairfield. *Art News* 50 (February 1952), p. 42. Exhibition at de Nagy Gallery, New York.

_____ . "Robert Goodnough." *Art News* 51 (November 1952), p. 45.

_____ . "Robert Goodnough." *Art News* 57 (January 1959), p. 10.

Preston, Stuart. "Contemporary Cross-Currents." *New York Times* (15 January 1961).

Raynor, Vivien. "Robert Goodnough." *Arts Magazine* 38 (March 1964), p. 67.

_____ . "Robert Goodnough." *Arts Magazine* 39 (May/June 1965), pp. 56-57.

Rose, Matthew. "Robert Goodnough." *Art Gallery International* 9 (March/April 1988), pp. 10-13.

Sandler, Irving H. "Robert Goodnough." *Art News* 58 (January 1960), p. 12.

_____ . "Robert Goodnough." *Art News* 59 (January 1961), p. 11.

_____ . "Robert Goodnough." *Art News* 62 (April 1963), p. 12.

Sawin, Martica. "Robert Goodnough." *Arts Digest* (15 May 1955), p. 29.

Schuyler, James. "Robert Goodnough." *Art News* 54 (January 1956), p. 51.

Steinberg, Leo. *Arts Magazine* 30 (January 1956), pp. 46-47. Exhibition of New York Painters at Stable Gallery.

Swenson, G.R. "Robert Goodnough" *Art News* 61 (March 1962), p. 12.

_____ . "Robert Goodnough." *Art News* 62 (February 1964), p. 8.

Tyler, Parker. "Robert Goodnough." *Art News* 56 (March 1957), p. 8.

_____ . "Robert Goodnough." *Art News* 56 (January 1958), p. 16.

Young, Vernon. "Robert Goodnough." *Arts Magazine* 31 (May 1957), p. 51.

Grace Hartigan

Books and Exhibition Catalogs

Art: A Woman's Sensibility. Valencia, California: Feminist Art Program, California Institute of the Arts, 1975.

Grace Hartigan. Easton, Pennsylvania: Van Wickle Gallery, Lafayette College, 1983.

Hartigan: Thirty Years of Painting. Fort Wayne, Indiana: Fort Wayne Museum of Art, 1981.

Munro, Eleanor. *Originals: American Women Artists*. New York: Simon and Schuster, 1979.

Peterson, Karen and Willson, J.J. *Women Artists: Recognition and Reappraisal, From the Early Middle Ages to the 20th Century*. New York: Harper and Row, 1976.

Periodicals

Art News 56 (March 1957), p. 31. Exhibition at de Nagy Gallery.

Ashton, Dore. *Kunstwerk* 16 (November 1962), p. 69. Exhibition at Martha Jackson Gallery.

Baur, J.I.H. "Eastern Artists." *Art in America* 42 (Winter 1954), no. 1, pp. 18-19.

Campbell, Lawrence. "Reviews and Previews: Grace Hartigan." *Art News* 54 (March 1955), pp. 51-2.

"Entering the Public Domain." *Pittsburgh Art News* 58 (May 1959), p. 37.

"Fifty-six Painters and Sculptors." *Art in America* 52 (August 1964), p. 31.

"Laurels for New Talent Artists of 1954 and 1955." *Art in America* 44 (February 1956), p. 59.

Preston, S. "Recent Work at the Martha Jackson Gallery." *Burlington Magazine* 104 (December 1962), p. 565.

Sandler, Irving. "Young Moderns and Modern Masters." *Art News* 56 (March 1957), pp. 31, 63.

Schwartz, M.D. "Hartigan at De Nagy Gallery." *Apollo* 70 (September 1959), p. 62.

Soby, James Thrall. "Non-abstract Authorities." *Saturday Review* (23 April 1955), pp. 52-3.

"Woman Artists in Ascendance." *Life* (13 May 1957), p. 75.

Zerner, H. *L'Oeil* no. 120 (December 1964), p. 38.

Lester Johnson

Books and Exhibition Catalogs

Chernow, Burt and Rosenberg, Harold. *Lester Johnson: The Kaleidoscopic Crowd, Paintings 1970-74*. New York: David Anderson Publications, 1975.

Contemporary Urban Visions. New York: New School Art Center, 1966.

Johnson, Lester. *The Devil's Front Porch*. Lawrence: University Press of Kansas, 1970.

Lester Johnson, Street Scenes. New York: Gimpel & Weitzenhoffer, 1980.

Ratcliff, Carter. *Lester Johnson: Recent Paintings*. Birmingham, Michigan: The Gallery, 1981.

Stein, Judith. *Lester Johnson*. New York: Gallery Moos Ltd., 1987.

Periodicals

Ashton, Dore. *Arts and Architecture* 78 (April 1961), pp. 4-5. Exhibition at Zabriskie Gallery.

_____ . "New York Exhibitions." *Arts and Architecture* 80 (January 1963), pp. 4-5.

_____ . "Show at the Martha Jackson Gallery." *Arts and Architecture* 83 (April 1966), pp. 6-7.

Bass, Ruth. "Lester Johnson." *Art News* 79 (September 1980), pp. 241-42.

_____ . "Lester Johnson." *Art News* 81 (October 1982), pp. 158, 160.

_____ . "Lester Johnson at Zabriskie." *Art News* 82 (December 1983), pp. 153-54.

Campbell, Lawrence. "Lester Johnson in the Bowery." *Art News* 62 (February 1964), pp. 47, 60-61.

Colt, Priscilla. "Remarks on the Figure and Lester Johnson." *Art International* 7 (January 1964), pp. 64-67.

"Combining Man and the Monument." *Time* (18 February 1966).

Genauer, Emily. "Korman Shows Johnson." *New York Herald Tribune* (6 February 1954).

Gruen, John. "Lester Johnson." *New York Magazine* (21 March 1971).

Mellow, James. "A Movement of Strength in Art by Lester Johnson." *New York Times* (3 March 1973).

Parrino, George. "A Talk with Lester Johnson." *The Soho Weekly News* (13 March 1975).

Pearlstein, Philip. "Private Myth, A Symposium." *Art News* 60 (September 1961), p. 42-45.

Rosenberg, Harold. "Images as Counterforce." *Art News* 64 (February 1966), pp. 48-49, 64.

_____ . "Johnson's Men." *The New Yorker* (18 February 1966).

Russell, John. "Lester Johnson's Outgoing People." *New York Times* (4 November 1977).

Schuyler, James. "Lester Johnson." *Art News* 57 (March 1958), p. 40.

Thompsen, Barbara. "The Individual as a Crowd: Lester Johnson's Recent Paintings." *Art in America* (November/December 1973).

Alex Katz

Books and Exhibition Catalogs

Alex Katz from the Early 60s. New York: Robert Miller Gallery, 1987.

Beattie, Ann. *Alex Katz*. New York: Harry N. Abrams, 1987.

Berkson, Bill and Sandler, Irving, eds. *Alex Katz*. New York: Praeger Publishers, 1971.

Marshall, Richard and Katz, Alex. *Alex Katz*. New York: Whitney Museum of American Art and Rizzoli Inernational Publications, 1986.

Sandler, Irving. *Alex Katz*. New York: Harry N. Abrams, 1979.

Periodicals

Barnitz, J. *Arts Magazine* 39 (February 1965), p. 59. Exhibition at Fischbach Gallery.

Denby, Edwin. "Katz: Collage, Cutout, Cut-Up." *Art News* 63 (January 1965), pp. 42-5.

Oeri, G. "Object of Art." *Quadrum* no. 16 (1964), p. 17.

Raynor, Vivien. *Arts Magazine* 38 (March 1964), p. 70. Exhibition at Thibaut Gallery.

_____ . *Arts Magazine* 36 (April 1962), p 59. Exhibition at Tanager Gallery.

Sandler, Irving H. "Alex Katz, 1957-1959." *Arts Magazine* 55 (February 1981), pp. 98-99. Exhibition at Robert Miller Gallery.

Schuyler, James. "Alex Katz Paints a Picture." *Art News* 60 (February 1962), pp. 38-41.

Tillim, Sidney. *Arts Magazine* 37 (April 1963), pp. 48-9. Exhibition at Thibaut Gallery.

_____ . "Katz Cocktail: Grand and Cozy." *Art News* 64 (December 1965), pp. 46-49. Exhibition at Fischback Gallery.

Unattributed/Untitled Reviews

Art News 49 (February 1949), p. 49. Exhibition at Peter Cooper Gallery.

Art News 52 (May 1953), p. 55. Exhibition at Tanager Gallery.

Art News 53 (November 1954), p. 66. Exhibition at Roko Gallery.

Art News 55 (January 1957), p. 55. Exhibition at Roko Gallery.

Art News 57 (January 1959), p. 15.

Exhibition at Tanager Gallery.

Art News 60 (February 1962), p. 14. Exhibition at Tanager Gallery.

Art News 61 (February 1963), p. 11. Exhibition at Thibaut Gallery.

Art News 61 (Summer 1962), p. 47. Exhibition at Jackson Gallery.

Art News 62 (February 1964), p. 9. Exhibition at Thibaut Gallery.

Arts Digest 27 (June 1953), p. 21. Exhibition at Tanager Gallery.

Arts Digest 29 (1 November 1954), p. 29. Exhibition at Roko Gallery.

Arts Magazine 31 (January 1957), p. 55. Exhibition at Roko Gallery.

George McNeil

Exhibition Catalogs

George McNeil: Expressionism 1954-1984. New York: Artists' Choice Museum, 1984.

George McNeil: Paintings. New York: Poindexter Gallery, 1957.

George McNeil: The Past Twenty Years. Fort Lauderdale, Florida: Museum of Art, 1982.

McNeil, George. "Good Painting," in *Painting as Painting*, pp. 6, 8, 10, 12. Austin: The Art Museum of the University of Texas at Austin, 1968.

The Painting of George McNeil. Austin: The University Art Museum of the University of Texas at Austin, 1966. Includes "Sensation and Modern Painting" by George McNeil.

Periodicals

Brenson, Michael. "Art: Expressionism and George McNeil." *New York Times* (5 October 1984).

Brown, Gordon. "In the Galleries: George McNeil." *Arts Magazine* 42 (November 1967), pp. 54-55.

Burton, Scott. "George McNeil and the Figure." *Art News* 66 (October 1967), pp. 38-39, 64.

Cameron, Dan. "Content in Context: The Retrospectives of Leon Golub and George McNeil." *Arts Magazine* 59 (March 1985), pp. 115-18.

Finkelstein, Louis. "'Cajori':The Figure in the Scene." *Art News* 62 (March 1963), p.39.

Freed, Leanor. "A Windfall for Texas." *Art in America* 55 (September/October 1967), p 84.

Glueck, Grace. "Think Up a New Brand Name?" *Art in America* 55 (September/October 1967), p. 111.

Goldin, Amy. "George McNeil." *Arts Magazine* 40 (April 1966), p. 69.

Greenberg, Clement. "New York Painting only Yesterday." *Art News* 56 (Summer 1957), p. 86.

Grove, Nancy. "George McNeil." *Arts Magazine* 50 (January 1976), p. 15.

Hess, Thomas B. "Is Abstraction Un-American?" *Art News* 49 (February 1951), p. 41.

Higgins, Judith. "Heroes of Myth and of The Morning After." *Art News* 85 (September 1986), pp. 90-99.

Kramer, Hilton. "Two Polemicists Respond to the Mood of the Times." *New York Times* (18 January 1981), Section D, pp. 23, 26.

Levin, Kim. "George McNeil." *Art News* 65 (March 1966), p. 17.

Newman, David. "George McNeil." *Arts Magazine* 55 (March 1981), p. 24.

Pomfret, Margaret. "George McNeil." *Arts Magazine* 52 (January 1978), p. 34.

Ratcliff, Carter. "George McNeil at Gruenebaum." *Art in America* 69 (May 1981), p. 145.

Rose, Barbara. "New York: George McNeil." *Artforum* (November 1967), pp. 58-60.

Rosenblum, Robert. "Editors Letters." *Art News* 60 (Summer 1961), p. 6.

Sandler, Irving H. "George McNeil." *Art News* 57 (January 1959), p. 12.

Schuyler, James. "George McNeil." *Art News* 55 (February 1957), pp. 9-10.

Jan Müller

Exhibition Catalogs

Exhibition of Paintings: 11th Annual Creative Arts Program. Boulder: University of Colorado, 1958.

Expansionists. New York: House of Duveen, 1951.

Jan Müller. New York: Hansa Gallery, 1958.

Jan Müller. New York: Oil & Steel Gallery, 1985.

Jan Müller. Bern, Switzerland: Stämpfli and Cie, 1964.

Jan Müller: 1922-1958. New York: Gruenebaum Gallery, Ltd., 1976.

Jan Müller, 1922-1958. New York: Solomon R. Guggenheim Foundation, 1962.

Jan Müller: Watercolors and Gouaches: 1950-54. New York: Zabriskie Gallery, 1961.

The Landscapes of Jan Müller. New York: Gruenebaum Gallery, 1977. Essay by Jeffrey Hoffeld.

Young America 1957: Thirty American Painters and Sculptors Under Thirty-five. New York, Whitney Museum of American Art, 1957.

Periodicals

Ashton, Dore. "Jan Müller" (New York Notes), *Art International* 5 (1 May 1961), p. 81.

_____ . "Jan Müller." *Arts Digest* 27 (1 April 1953), pp. 20, 24.

"Airless Despair." *Time* (2 February 1962).

Campbell, Lawrence. "Jan Müller" (Reviews and Previews). *Art News* 54 (February 1956), p. 51. Exhibition at Hansa Gallery.

_____ . "Jan Müller" (Reviews and Previews). *Art News* 57 (December 1958), p. 16. Exhibition at Hansa Gallery.

_____ . "Seven Shows for Spring, '61." *Art News* 60 (April 1961), pp. 47, 60.

"Five Star Shows this Winter." *Art News* 60 (February 1962), p. 44.

Frankfurter, Alfred. "The Voyages of Dr. Caligari Through Time and Space." *Art News* 55 (January 1957), pp. 31, 65.

Judd, Donald. *Arts Magazine* 36 (February 1962), p. 46. *813 Broadway* exhibition at Zabriskie Gallery.

Porter, Fairfield. "Jan Müller" (News and Previews). *Art News* 52 (March 1953), p. 55.

_____ . "Jan Müller" (Reviews and Previews). *Art News* 53 (April 1954), pp. 47, 53.

Rudikoff, Sonya. "Images in Painting." *Arts Magazine* 34 (June 1960), pp. 41-42, 45.

Sawin, Martica. "Jan Müller: 1922-1958." *Arts Magazine* 33 (February 1959), pp. 38-45.

_____ . "Jan Müller" (Fortnight in Review). *Arts Digest* 29 (15 April 1955), p. 20.

_____ . "Jan Müller" (In the Galleries). *Arts Magazine* 31 (January 1957), p. 51.

Tillim, Sidney. *Arts Magazine* 37 (January 1963), p. 51. Exhibition at Zabriskie Gallery.

Unattributed/Untitled Reviews

Art News 54 (May 1955), pp. 51, 56.

Art News 56 (January 1958), pp. 16-17.

Art News 60 (December 1961), p. 13. *Broadway* 813 at Zabriskie Gallery.

Art News 61 (January 1963), p. 11. Exhibition at Zabriskie Gallery.

Arts Magazine 30 (February 1956), p. 58.

Arts Magazine 32 (January 1958), p. 53.

Arts Magazine 35 (April 1961), p. 51. Exhibition at Zabriskie Gallery.

Jackson Pollock

Books and Exhibition Catalogs

Busignani, Alberto. *Pollock*. London, New York, Hamlyn: 1971. (Series title: Twentieth-century Masters).

Frank, Elizabeth. *Jackson Pollock*. New York: Abbeville Press, 1983. (Modern Masters Series.)

Friedman, B.H. *Jackson Pollock: Energy Made Visible*. New York: McGraw-Hill, 1972.

Gagnon, Francois-Marc. *Jackson Pollock: Questions*. Montreal: Ministere des affaires culturelles, Musée d'art contemporain, 1979.

Hunter, Sam. *Jackson Pollock*. New York: The Museum of Modern Art, 1956.

Jackson Pollock et la nouvelle peinture americaine. Paris: Musée national d'art moderne, 1959.

Jackson Pollock: Paintings, Drawings and Watercolors from the Collection of Lee Krasner Pollock. London: Marlborough Fine Art Ltd., 1961.

Kambartel, Walter. *Jackson Pollock, Number 32, 1950*. Stuttgart: Reclam, 1970.

Lieberman, William S. *Jackson Pollock, The Last Sketch Book*. New York: Johnson Reprint Corp./Harcourt Brace Jovanovich, 1982.

Namuth, Hans, ed. *L'atelier de Jackson Pollock*. Paris: Macula/Pierre Brochet, 1978.

O'Connor, Francis. *Jackson Pollock*. New York: The Museum of Modern Art, 1967.

_____ and Thaw, Eugene Victor, eds. *Jackson Pollock: A Catalogue Raisonné of Paintings, Drawings, and Other Works*. New Haven: Yale University Press, 1978. Three volumes.

O'Hara, Frank. *Jackson Pollock*. New York: George Braziller, 1959.

_____ . *Jackson Pollock*. New York: Harry N. Abrams, 1960.

Potter, Jeffrey, ed. *To a Violent Grave: An Oral Biography of Jackson Pollock*. New York: G.P. Putham, 1985.

Rohn, Matthew. *Visual Dynamics in Jackson Pollock's Abstractions*. Anne Arbor, Michigan: UMI Research Press, 1987.

Rose, Barbara. *Krasner/Pollock, A Working Relationship*. East Hampton, New York: Guild Hall Museum, 1981.

_____ , ed. *Pollock Painting/Photos*. New York: Agrinde Publications, 1980.

Rose, Bernice. *Jackson Pollock, Drawing into Painting*. New York: Museum of Modern Art, 1980.

Solomon, Deborah. *Jackson Pollock: A Biography*. New York: Simon and Schuster, 1987.

Periodicals

Alloway, Lawrence. "The Art of Jackson Pollock: 1912-1956." *The Listener* (BBC journal) 60 (27 November 1958), p. 888.

_____ . "Notes on Pollock." *Art International* 5 (May 1961), pp. 38-41.

_____ . "Sign and Surface: Notes on Black and White Painting in New York." *Quadrum* no. 9 (1960), pp. 51-2.

Ashton, Dore. "Exhibition of Fifteen Years of Work at the Sidney Jannis Gallery." *Arts and Architecture* 73 (January 1956), p. 10.

Coates, R.M. "Art Galleries: Balthus and Pollock at the Museum of Modern Art." *The New Yorker* (29 December 1956), pp. 47-9.

"Confrontation internationale: la deux-ieme exposition Documenta organisée au Museum Fridericianum de Cassel." *L'Oeil* no. 57 (September 1959), p. 22.

Friedman, B.H. "Profile: Jackson Pollock." *Art in America* 43 (December

1955), pp. 49, 58-9.

Goodnough, Robert. "Pollock Paints a Picture." *Art News* 50 (May 1951), pp. 38-41.

Hess, Thomas B. "Jackson Pollock, 1912-56." *Art News* 55 (September 1956), pp. 44-5.

_____ . "Pollock: The Art of a Myth." *Art News* 62 (January 1964), pp. 39-41. Reply by R. Browne, February 1964, p. 6.

"Jackson Pollock and the New American Painting at the Musée d'Art Moderne." *Art News* 58 (March 1959), p. 47.

"Jackson Pollock, Is He the Greatest Living Painter in the United States?" *Life* (8 August 1949), pp. 42-5.

Kaprow, A. "The Legacy of Jackson Pollock." *Art News* 57 (October 1958), pp. 24-6.

_____ . "Impurity." *Art News* 61 (January 1963), p. 53.

Kramer, Hilton. "Month in Review." *Arts Magazine* 31 (February 1957), pp. 46-8.

Lavin. "Abstraction in Modern Painting: A Comparison." *Metropolitan Museum of Art Bulletin* 19 (February 1961), pp. 166-71.

O'Connor, Francis. "Jackson Pollock: 1912 to 1943." *Artforum* 5 (May 1967), pp. 16-23.

Pollock, Jackson. "Answers to a Questionnaire." *Arts and Architecture* (February 1944).

"Pollock Throwing Skeins of Enamel." *Art News* 51 (June 1952), p. 66.

Rexroth, Kenneth. "Americans Seen Abroad." *Art News* 58 (June 1959), pp. 30-3.

Robertson, B. "Jackson Pollock." *Art News* 59 (February 1961), p. 35.

Rubin, William. "Jackson Pollock and the Modern Tradition," Parts I-IV. *Artforum* 5 (February 1967), pp. 14-22; (March

1967), pp. 28-37; (April 1967), pp. 18-31; (May 1967), pp. 28-33.

_____ . "Notes on Masson and Pollock." *Arts Magazine* 34 (November 1959), pp. 36-43.

Steinberg, Leo. "Fifteen Years Work Shown at the Sidney Janis Gallery." *Arts Magazine* 30 (December 1955), pp. 43-4.

Strauss, M. "Major Exhibition of Paintings and Drawings at Marlborough Fine Art." *Burlington Magazine* 103 (July 1961), p. 327.

Sweeny, J.J. "Five American Painters." *Harper's Bazaar* (April 1944).

Tillim, Sidney. "Jackson Pollock, A Critical Evaluation." *College Art Journal* 16 (1957), pp. 242-3.

_____ . *Arts Magazine* 38 (March 1964), pp. 55-6. Retrospective at the Marlborough-Gerson Gallery.

Tyler, Parker. "Jackson Pollock: The Infinite Labryrinth." *Magazine of Art* 43 (March 1950), pp. 92-3.

_____ . "Pollock." *Art News Annual* 26 (1957), pp. 86-107.

Valiere, J.T. "El Greco Influence on Jackson Pollock's Early Works." *Art Journal* 24 (Fall 1964), pp. 6-9.

"The Wild Ones." *Time* (20 February 1956), pp. 70-1.

Unattributed/Untitled Reviews

Art News 51 (December 1952), p. 42. Exhibition at Sidney Janis Gallery.

Arts and Architecture 71 (March 1954), p. 7. Exhibition at at Sidney Janis Gallery.

Arts Digest 27 (November 1952), p. 16. Exhibition at Sidney Janis Gallery.

Arts Magazine 32 (May 1958), pp. 22-3. Five Americans at the Institute of Contemporary Arts.

Burlington Magazine 99 (February 1957), p. 68. Retrospective at Museum of Modern Art, New York.

Fairfield Porter

Books and Exhibition Catalogs

Ashberry, John and Moffett, Kenworth. *Fairfield Porter: A Realist Painter in an Age of Abstraction*. Boston: Museum of Fine Arts, 1982.

Downes, Rackstraw. *Fairfield Porter— Figurative Painting*. New York: Hirschl & Adler Galleries, 1979.

Ludman, Joan. *Fairfield Porter: A Catalogue Raisonné of His Prints, including Illustrations, Bookjackets, and Exhibition Posters*. Westbury, New York: Highland House, 1981.

Periodicals

"Art as a History of Drawing." *Art News* 58 (December 1959), p. 44.

Beem, E.A. "People and Things Connected—Fairfield Porter, Curator and Critic." *Portland Independent* (Portland, Maine), 27 July 1979.

Benedikt, M. "Fairfield Porter: Minimum of Melodrama." *Art News* 63 (March 1964), pp. 36-7

"Fairfield Porter: An American Classic." *The New Criterion* (May 1983), p. 5.

Kramer, Hilton. "Porter—A Virtuoso

Colorist." *New York Times* (25 November 1979).

_____ . "Portraiture, The Living Art." *Harper's Bazaar* (March 1981).

Lanes, J. "Fairfield Porter's Recent Work." *Arts Magazine* 38 (April 1964), pp. 40-43.

"Meeting Ground at the Whitney." *Art News* 55 (May 1956), pp. 38-9.

O'Hara, Frank. "Porter Paints a Picture: Portrait of Katharine." *Art News* 53 (January 1955), pp. 38-41.

Porter, Fairfield. *Arts Magazine* 39 (October 1964), p. 6. Reply with rejoinder to Lane's "Fairfield Porter's Recent Work."

Larry Rivers

Books and Exhibition Catalogs

Haenlein, Carl, ed. *Larry Rivers, Retrospektive: Bilder und Skulpturen*. Hannover, West Germany: Kestner-Gesellschaft, 1980.

Harrison, Helen A. *Larry Rivers*. New York: Harper and Row, 1984.

_____ . *Larry Rivers, Performing for the Family*. East Hampton, New York: Guild Hall Museum, 1983.

Hunter, Sam. *Larry Rivers*. New York: Harry N. Abrams, 1972.

_____ . *Larry Rivers*. New York: Published for the Poses Institute of Fine Arts, Brandeis University, by October House, 1970.

Larry Rivers: The Continuing Interest in Abstract Art. New York: Marlborough Gallery, 1981.

Rivers, Larry and Brightman, Carol. *Drawings and Digressions*. New York: Clarkson N. Potter, Inc./Crown Publishers, 1979.

Rosenzweig, Phyllis. *Larry Rivers: The H.M. & S.G. Collection*. Washington, D.C.: Hirshhorn Museum and Sculpture Garden, Smithsonian Institution Press, 1981.

Soby, James Thrall. Modern Art and the New Past, pp. 192-96. Norman: University of Oklahoma Press, 1957.

Periodicals

Arts Magazine 32 (December 1958), p. 60.

Ashbery, John. "Paris Letter." *Art International* (1 April 1962), p. 61.

Berkson, William. "The Sculpture of Larry Rivers." *Arts Magazine* 40 (November 1965), pp. 49-52.

Brookner, Anita. "Current and Forthcoming Exhibitions: London." *Burlington Magazine* 104 (July 1962), p. 314.

Burr, J. "Larry Rivers." *Arts Review* (London) (2-16 May 1964), p. 4.

Calas, Nicolas. "Larry Rivers." *Art International* (1 March 1961), pp. 36-39.

Campbell, Lawrence. *Art News* 56 (December 1957), p. 11.

_____ . *Art News* 59 (February 1961), p. 15.

Canady, John. "Of Two Painters: Rivers and Roth." *New York Times* (9 December 1962), Section 2, p. 17.

_____ . "Art: Larry Rivers Juxtaposing the High and Low." *New York Times* (26 August 1963), p. 21.

_____ . "N.Y. Sees Paintings by Rivers." *New York Times* (27 September 1965), p. 5.

Coates, Robert M. "The Art Galleries: Variations on a Theme." *New Yorker* (23 December 1961), p. 62.

"Creative Process." *Arts Digest* 28 (15 January 1954), pp. 15-6.

De Kooning, Elaine. *Art News* 48 (April 1949), p. 47.

Farber, Manny. "Art." *The Nation* (13 October 1951), pp. 313-14.

Glueck, Grace. "Larry Rivers Paints Himself into the Canvas." *New York Times Magazine* (13 February 1965), pp. 34-35, 78-83.

_____ . "Art Notes: A Rivers Introspective." *New York Times* (31 October 1965), Section 2, p. 29.

Goodnough, Robert. *Art News* 51 (December 1952), p. 44.

Gowing, Lawrence. "Painters to Watch—6: Larry Rivers." *Observer* (London) (4 December 1960).

Grantz, Roberta B. "Closeup: An Artist Looks Back." *New York Post* (13 October 1965).

Greenberg, Clement. "Art." *The Nation* (26 April 1949), pp. 453-54.

Hess, Thomas B. "Larry Rivers' History of the Russian Revolution." *Art News* 64 (October 1965), pp. 36-7.

Holliday, Betty. *Art News* 50 (October 1951), p. 47.

Hunter, Sam. "Recent Work of Larry Rivers." *Arts Magazine* 39 (April 1965), 44-50.

_____ . "Larry Rivers." *Quadrum* no. 18 (1965), pp. 99-114, 183-84.

"Jam Session." *Newsweek* (26 April 1965), p. 65.

Kozloff, Max. "Art." *The Nation* (23 December 1961), pp. 519-20.

_____ . "New York Notes." *Art International* (1 February 1962), p. 71.

Kramer, Hilton. "Season's Gleanings: Toward 'Pop' with Larry Rivers." *Art in America* 51 (June 1963), p. 136.

Mastai, M.S.D. "Flats, Shoes, Buicks and Websters." *Apollo* (July 1961), p. 197.

Porter, Fairfield. "Rivers Paints a Picture: Portrait of Berdie." *Art News* 52 (January 1954), pp. 56-9.

_____ . *Art News* 57 (December 1958), p. 14.

Preston, Stuart. "Rivers: Out of the Abstract into the Real." *New York Times* (11 December 1954), p. 11.

"Quipster." *Time* (16 April 1965), pp. 94-5.

Reichardt, J. "Worsdell, Waters and Rivers at Woodstock Gallery." *Apollo* 75 (July 1961), p. 24.

Rosenberg, Harold. "Rivers' Commedia dell'Arte." *Art News* 64 (April 1965), pp. 35-37, 62.

Sandler, Irving H. "New York Letter." *Quadrum* no. 14 (1963), pp. 120-1.

_____ . *Art News* 60 (December 1961), p. 11.

_____ . "New York Letter." *Art International* (1 February 1961), pp. 34-35.

_____ . "New York Letter." *Quadrum* no. 14 (1963), pp. 120-21.

Sawin, Martica. "In the Galleries." *Arts Magazine* 31 (December 1956), p. 55.

Schneider, P. "*Art News from Paris.*" *Art News* 61 (Summer 1962), pp. 42-3.

Seckler, D.G. "Artist in America: Victim of the Culture Boom?" *Art in America* 51 (December 1963), pp. 28-33.

Steinberg, Leo. "Month in Review: Contemporary Group of New York Painters at Stable Gallery." *Arts Magazine* 30 (January 1956), p. 48.

Tillim, Sidney. *Arts Magazine* 36 (February 1962), p. 41. Exhibition at Tibor de Nagy Gallery.

Tyler, Parker. "Purple Patch of Fetishism." *Art News* 56 (March 1957), pp. 40-43.

"Two Sculptors, Two Painters for December." *Art News* 59 (December 1960), pp. 40-43.

Whittet, G.S. "You Can't Write Off the British: London Commentary." *Studio International* no. 164 (August 1962), p. 75.

Wilson, William. "Larry Rivers: Pasadena Art Museum." *Artforum* (October 1965), p. 13.

"Wonder Boy and His Many Sides." *Life* (October 1958), p. 100.

"Young Draftsman on Master Draftsman." *Art News* 53 (January 1955), pp. 26-7.

Bob Thompson

Books and Exhibition Catalogs

Dillinberger, Jane and John. *Perceptions of the Spirit in Twentieth-Century American Art*. Indianapolis, Indiana: Indianapolis Museum of Art, 1977.

Fine, Elsa Honig. *The Afro-American Artist: A Search for Identity*. New York: Holt, Rinehart & Winston, 1973.

Geldzahler, Henry. *Underknown: Twelve Artists Re-seen in 1984*. Long Island City, New York: The Institute for Art and Urban Resources, 1984.

Ghent, Henri. *8 artistes afro-americains*. Geneva, Switzerland: Musée Rath, 1971.

Igoe, Lynn Moody. *250 Years of Afro-American Art: An Annotated Bibliography*. New York: R.R. Bowker, Co. 1981.

Lerner, Abram, ed. *The Hirshhorn Museum and Sculpture Garden*. New York: Harry N. Abrams, 1974.

Lewis, Samella. *Art: African American*. New York: Harcourt Brace Jovanovich, 1978.

Miller-Keller, Andrea. *Bob Thompson: MATRIX 90*. Hartford Connecticut: Wadsworth Atheneum, 1986.

Nelson Stevens, et. al. *Bob Thompson*. Amherst, Massachusetts: University Art Gallery, University of Massachusetts at Amherst.

Richter, Horace and Schapiro, Meyer. *The Horace Richter Collection: Contemporary American Painting and Sculpture*. Charlotte, North Carolina: The Mint Museum of Art, 1960.

Schapiro, Meyer, et al. *Bob Thompson 1937-1966*. Louisville, Kentucky: J.B. Speed Art Museum, 1966.

Teilhet, Jehanne, ed. *Dimensions of Black*. La Jolla, California: La Jolla Museum of Art, 1970.

Wight, Frederick and Porter, James A. *The Negro in American Art*. Los

Angeles: UCLA Art Galleries, Dickson
Art Center, University of California, 1966.

Wilson, Judith and Miller, William P., Jr.
Bob Thompson. Jamaica, New York:
Jamaica Arts Center, 1987.

Periodicals

Harrison, J. *Arts Magazine* 38 (February
1964), Exhibition at Drawing Shop and
Jackson Galleries.

Unattributed/Untitled Reviews

Art News 58 (February 1960), p. 19.
Exhibition at Delancey Street Museum.

Art News 59 (Summer 1960), p. 18.
Exhibition at Zabriskie Gallery.

Art News 59 (November 1960), p. 19.
Exhibition in New York.

Art News 62 (December 1963), p. 50.
Exhibition at Drawing Shop Gallery.

Art News 62 (January 1964), p. 15.
Exhibition at Jackson Gallery.

Arts Magazine 34 (Suumer 1960), p. 59.
Exhibition at Zabriskie Gallery.

Arts Magazine 35 (December 1960), p.
58. Exhibition at City Gallery.

Compiled by Katherine Hovde.
Bob Thompson material provided
by Judith Wilson.

Photo Credits

Plates

Rudolph Burchkhardt: cat. 25; Carlo Catenazzi: cat. 10; Geoffrey Clements: cats. 32, 44, 53, 69, 71; eeva-inkeri: cat. 41; Tom Feist: cat. 19; Rick Harman: cat. 36; David Heald: cats. 48, 55; Biff Henrich: cat. 24; George Holmes: cat. 3; Bill Jacobson: cat. 52; Paulus Leeser: cat. 61; Edvard Lieber: cats. 5 through 8, 25; Paul Macapia: cat. 23; Michael McKelvey: cat. 60; Otto E. Nelson: cat. 13; William Nettles: cat. 16; Gene Ogami: cats. 15, 51; Eric Pollitzer: cat. 50; Copyright © Larry Rivers/VAGA, N.Y., 1988: cats. 67 through 75; David Rosselli: cat. 22; Noel Rowe: cat. 57, 58; Lee Stalsworth: cat. 20; Joseph Szasfai: cat. 76; Will Thornton: cat. 11; David Wharton, copyright © ARS N.Y./Pollock-Krasner Foundation, 1988: cat. 56

Essay Photos

Yvonne Andersen: p. 42 top; Copyright © ARS, N.Y./Pollock-Krasner Foundation, 1988: p. 48; Copyright © ARS, N.Y./Succession H. Matisse, 1988: p. 18 top; Copyright © Bild-Kunst/VAGA, N.Y., 1988: p. 20 top; Rudolph Burckhardt, © Larry Rivers/VAGA, N.Y., 1988: p. 148; Allan Finkelman, Courtesy Sidney Janis Gallery: p. 42 bottom; Jim Frank, copyright © ARS, N.Y./Milton Avery Trust, 1988: p. 23 top; Robert E. Mates, copyright © ARS, N.Y./ADAGP, 1988: p. 21 bottom; Colin McRae: p. 39; Copyright © Larry Rivers/VAGA, N.Y., 1988: p. 45 left; Sunami, copyright © ARS, N.Y./ADAGP/SPADEM, 1988: p. 18 bottom; Joesph Szasfai, copyright © ARS, N.Y./SPADEM, 1988: p. 19 bottom.